First Peter
Faith refined by fire

by David Schroeder

Faith and Life
Bible Studies

Faith and Life Press
Newton, Kansas

These [trials] have come so that your faith—of greater worth than gold, which perishes even though refined by fire—may be proved genuine and may result in praise, glory and honor when Jesus Christ is revealed (1 Peter 1:7, New International Version).

Copyright © 1985 by Faith and Life Press, Newton, Kansas 67114
Printed in the United States of America
Library of Congress Number 85-80428
International Standard Book Number 0-87303-103-2

The publishers gratefully acknowledge the support and encouragement of the Congregational Resources Board of the Conference of Mennonites in Canada in the development of this book.

Design by John Hiebert
Printing by Mennonite Press, Inc.

Faith refined by fire

Table of contents

Introduction

I invite you to study an exciting book with me. It shows that God's gift of new life brings changes to our everyday way of living. Peter speaks to issues real in his own time. Our situation may not be the same but that makes it all the more exciting and challenging because we then have to translate the message into our settings.

The study has two parts.

1. On the left page, I have introduced each portion of Scripture briefly and then asked some questions with which you might want to approach the biblical text itself. You should have the New International Version (NIV) Bible open to 1 Peter. Write your answers in the blank spaces provided. Do not rush your study. You may want to spend extra time on some lessons.

2. On the right page, I have given some additional information. Sometimes it is information about a word, a place, a person, or the author. At other times, I have given historical background material from the Old Testament, the intertestamental period, or the time of Jesus. I have also provided a few remarks on some important issues.

3. A third part is missing which you can supply. Apply these verses to your own life. Every now and then, I have asked questions of a practical kind but you have to supply the answer. Even where a question is not asked di-

rectly, you should always ask: What does this imply for us in our day?

How to begin

1. Conduct your own spiritual exercises first. We need to be in a proper frame of mind to be able to receive insight and inspiration from the Scriptures. Prepare to center your mind and energy on the study of 1 Peter. Shut out, as much as possible, outside intrusions. Open yourself through meditation and prayer to the author's word. Stop reading here and *do* it.

2. Drink in the message of 1 Peter by reading it in its entirety as if it were a letter sent to you by a caring friend. Read it as a letter. Read it aloud if possible. Don't stop to analyze its content. If there are things you don't understand, keep on reading. Stop here and read the letter.

3. Once you have read it, close your eyes and focus your thoughts on what the letter has communicated to you. Search out what was important to the author: What did he want to say? Why did he use these words? What seems most important for you?

4. Now start with the study for Session 1.

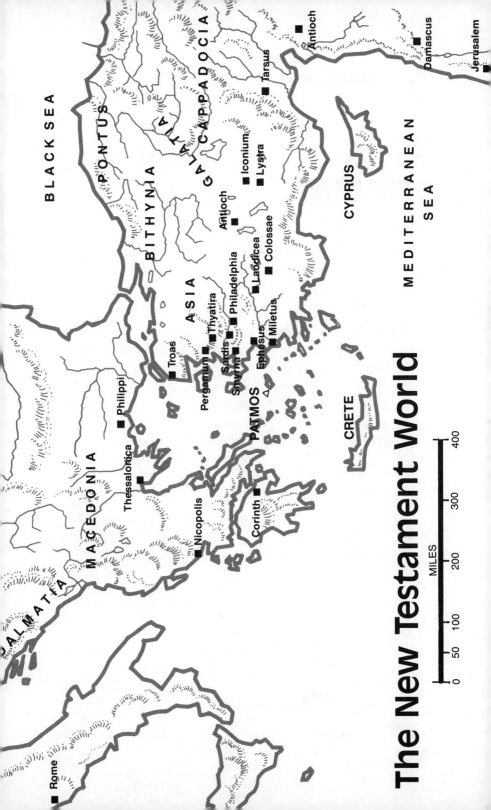

The New Testament World

BLACK SEA

MEDITERRANEAN SEA

CYPRUS

CRETE

PONTUS

BITHYNIA

GALATIA

CAPPADOCIA

ASIA

MACEDONIA

DALMATIA

Antioch

Damascus

Jerusalem

Tarsus

Iconium

Lystra

Antioch

Laodicea

Colossae

Philadelphia

Thyatira

Troas

Pergamum

Sardis

Smyrna

Ephesus

Miletus

PATMOS

Philippi

Thessalonica

Nicopolis

Corinth

Rome

MILES

0   50   100   200   300   400

Part I. Greetings

Session 1. Chosen strangers

1 Peter 1:1-2

The opening of this letter follows the usual form of a Greek or Latin letter. It gives the writer's name and the writer's office. It identifies the people receiving the letter and gives a proper greeting. The simplest greeting would be "[author's name] to [reader's name] greeting." First Peter 1:1-2 represents an expanded version of this form in that each of the three parts is expanded and given a specific Christian content.

1. Who is the author of the letter?

Name _____

His office or authority _____

2. The meaning of the word "apostle" is the "sent one." Insert "sent one" instead of "apostle" in 1:1. How does this identify the author as "servant" (1:1)?

_____

3. What were the qualifications of an apostle according to Acts 1:21-22?

_____

_____

4. Whose servant is Peter (1:1)?

How is his master identified? _____

_____

Greetings

The salutation takes the familiar Hebrew greeting "Peace" (Shalom) and combines it with the traditional Greek greeting "Grace" as a single greeting to these churches consisting of Jewish and Gentile Christians.

Peter, an apostle

The reference to Peter as an apostle of Jesus Christ (1:1) highlights two things: (1) he speaks as one who is sent by and represents Jesus Christ; (2) he lets the reader know that Jesus, about whom they have heard, is the Messiah, the Christ, who had been announced by the prophets.

The apostle Peter was one of the twelve disciples and is often mentioned along with James and John. His original name was Simon (Acts 15:14). The name "Petros" (Rock) was given to him by Jesus (Mark 3:16) and the Greek version of his Aramaic name was "Cephas" (John 1:42) which is used most often by Paul (1 Cor. 1:12; 3:22; Gal. 1:18; 2:9, 11, 14 [RSV]).

The father's name was Jonah (Matt. 16:17). His father and family were from the city of Bethsaida (John 1:44) and they were fishermen by trade. When Peter and his brother Andrew met Jesus they were probably living in Capernaum. It was actually Andrew who brought Peter to Jesus (John 1:41).

Peter was very active as a follower of Jesus. He is often

The writer

The writer does not say very much about himself, but if we look carefully at what he does say, we can at least get some impression of him. To study the Gospels in detail would, of course, give us even more information.

1. What relationship does the author have to the following people?

a. The elders (5:1) _____

b. The readers (5:1, 2:11) _____

c. Silas (5:12-14) _____

d. Mark (5:13) _____

2. What does the writer say about himself in the following verses where he uses the words "we" and "us"?

1:3 _____

2:24 _____

3:18 (RSV) _____

4:17 _____

3. Sometimes the author's references to himself are somewhat veiled or indirect. Read the verse in the left-hand column and note the possible reference to events which the apostle witnessed and which are reported in the Gospels.

1:3   Peter witnessed the resurrection of Jesus, i.e. found the tomb to be empty (John 20:3-9).

1:7-8   Peter saw the Lord yet denied him. His hearers had not seen Jesus but loved him.

1:10-12   After the resurrection Jesus told the apostles what was written about him in the Scriptures (Luke 24:45-46).

2:4   Jesus, during his earthly ministry, spoke about the rejected stone (Matt. 21:42).

2:20-25   This reads almost like an eyewitness account of the crucifixion.

mentioned and is usually listed first when the names of the disciples are given. He was married and later his wife accompanied him on his missionary tours (Mark 1:30; 1 Cor. 9:5).

Sometimes you might want to take a Bible dictionary and look up the article on "Peter." It tells about the experiences Peter had in following Jesus and in establishing the Christian church.

The writer of the letter

Some interpreters of 1 Peter question whether the apostle Peter wrote this letter. They find it hard to believe that he did for several reasons: (1) It is written in excellent, almost classical, Greek with a wide choice of words. It is felt that Peter, a fisherman, would not have been capable of this style of writing. (2) Some interpreters think that the sufferings referred to in this letter were caused by an official state persecution. Such persecutions took place only after Peter's death.

These objections to Petrine authorship are often answered by suggesting: (1) that Silvanus, to whom reference is made in the letter (5:12 Silas), was the secretary of Peter and did the actual writing using his own style and (2) that the persecution and suffering referred to were not caused by official government action against the Christians but were difficulties suffered at the hands of fellow citizens.

The people of the Dispersion

The writer refers to the hearers as "strangers in the world" and as "scattered" among the nations. It refers to a people living in the midst of other peoples. It was known in Judaism as the *Dispersion* or the *Diaspora*.

There may have been early, voluntary "dispersions" of Israel in that we read of a colony of Israelites in Damascus (1 Kings 20:34). The forced dispersions began with Assyrian and Babylonian domination. Their kings used

5:1-2, 4   Do these words not reflect the words of Jesus
            where he said, "Feed my Sheep"? (John 21:15-
            19).

The hearers

The hearers too are identified, but in language that
sounds strange to us. These words have a long history.
They were used to describe Israel in the Old Testament
and the people of God in the time of Jesus. Our knowledge of the hearers is largely restricted to information
given in the letter.

1. What is said about the hearers in the following passages?

1:1 _____

1:6 _____

1:8 _____

1:14 _____

1:18 _____

2:2 _____

2:9 _____

2:10 _____

2:11-12 _____

2:18 _____

2:25 _____

3:1 _____

3:14 _____

4:3 _____

4:4 _____

4:12 _____

the policy of displacing large numbers of the peoples conquered in war. Some of the people taken to Babylon in
588 B.C. in this way were later allowed to return to Jerusalem by Cyrus the Persian ruler.

After the time of Alexander the Great (323 B.C.), Jewish immigrants found their way to many countries such
as Syria, Asia Minor, Greece, and Rome. Wherever there
were ten heads of households a synagogue would be set
up to teach their children, and other people as well,
about the faith of Israel.

When Christian missionaries proclaimed the gospel in
these territories, they went first to the synagogues to
proclaim Jesus as Lord and Savior. In this letter, these
new Christians are seen as the people "scattered among
the nations." Jew and Gentile Christians now lived as
one people in the midst of people of other faiths.

The elect and chosen of God

Peter calls the Christians to whom he is writing the
"elect" of God. He knows full well that the children of
Israel were called the elect of God. The word "elect"
means that God chose a person or a nation for a purpose
of his own choosing. Thus, just as God chose Israel for a
specific purpose (to reveal who God is to the nations), so
God has chosen the Christians to be his own people to
make known "the praises of him who called" them (2:9).
The people of God in the Old Testament (Israel) and the
people of God in the New Testament (Christians) have a
common bond. Both are spoken of in terms of God's
choice or election.

The apostle indicates that they were *chosen* "according
to the foreknowledge of God the Father" (1:2); that they
were *sanctified* (made holy) and set apart for Christian
service by the Holy Spirit; and that this was done so that
they might become *obedient* to Jesus Christ who saved
them through his death on the cross. They were chosen
for a purpose.

4:16 _____

5:1 _____

2. On the basis of the above, indicate what you feel to be the three most important items mentioned about the hearers.

_____

_____

_____

3. Were the hearers (1) Jewish Christians, (2) Gentile Christians, or (3) both? Study the following references and see if you can decide.

1:1   Speaks of "strangers in the world" (NIV)—"exiles of the Dispersion" (RSV). This links the Christians with the Jews dispersed among the nations.

2:18   Speaks of "slaves" but we seldom hear of a class of slaves among the Jewish people.

4:3   They once walked in "darkness" or in "ignorance" (1:14).

1:10-12   Assumes they know the Old Testament prophets.

2:1-10   Speaks about Old Testament priesthood and sacrifices.

What is your conclusion? (Check one.) 1 ___ 2 ___ 3 ___

4. What statements are made in 1:2 about the Christian's relationship?

a. To God the Father _____

_____

b. To the Holy Spirit _____

_____

c. To Jesus Christ _____

_____

Peter and Rome

The church historian, Eusebius, says that Peter visited Rome in the reign of Claudius (A.D. 41-54). Peter may have fled to Rome to escape from Herod's persecution (Acts 12:1, 18, 19). Eusebius also tells us that Peter was executed with Paul in the reign of Nero (A.D. 54-68).

By way of summary

The apostle Peter is concerned about the suffering experienced by Christians at the hands of their fellow citizens. He directs his letter to these new converts who may think it strange that they are called upon to suffer for obeying the truth and for doing good.

The writer encourages these Christians by putting them into the stream of God's work with his people (as the elect) and by showing them that the sufferings are "for a little while" only. Besides, Christ also suffered in like manner. Therefore they are to purify and sanctify themselves through obedience to Christ so that their work and lifestyle may be observed by others (2:11-12) and that this will be their witness to Christ.

We will now have to see how this message develops.

5. What does each member of the Godhead do according to 1:2?

a. The Father _____

_____

b. The Spirit _____

_____

c. The Son _____

_____

6. For what purpose were the Christians chosen?

"For _____ to Jesus Christ. . ." (1:2).

7. With what words does the apostle greet the hearers (1:2)?

"_____ and _____ be yours in abundance."

Where was the letter sent?

The letter seems to have been sent as a circular letter to the churches in a larger area. The order in which the provinces are named suggests that the bearer of the letter started in the north and traveled in a clockwise direction through Asia Minor. (See map.) This geographic area represents a mixture of peoples—old native peoples, the more cultured Greeks, and oriental peoples as well as Jewish groups. The region was mixed not only in terms of race and culture, but also in terms of religious and political orientation. The Christian church was relatively new to the region but we have no direct statements about how these churches came into being.

1. List the places to which the letter was sent, and locate them on the map on page 1.

a. _____

b. _____

c. _____

The Greetings (1 Peter 1:1-2)

1:1

1:2

Peter
- an apostle
- of Jesus Christ

God
- Father (foreordains)
- Spirit (sanctifies)
- Son (sacrificial death)

Hearers
- God's elect/chosen
- Exiles/scattered
- Sanctified
- Obedient

Scattered in
- Pontus
- Galatia
- Cappadocia
- Asia
- Bithynia

Comments, additions:

d. _____

e. _____

   2. Can you venture some guesses as to how the Christian faith may have come to these regions?

_____

_____

   3. Is "she who is at Babylon" a possible reference to the church at the place from which the letter was written (5:13)? (See comment on "Peter and Rome.")

   4. Note the diagram of the greeting on the previous page. Write in any observations or thoughts you would like to remember.

Session notes

_____

_____

_____

_____

_____

_____

_____

_____

_____

_____

_____

_____

_____

_____

_____

_____

_____

_____

_____

_____

_____

_____

_____

_____

_____

Part II. A people belonging to God (1:3—2:10)

Session 2. New birth into a living hope

1 Peter 1:3-12

The apostle begins with an important statement. It is a statement that is basic to the entire letter and explains what the gospel (the good news) is all about. It refers to the good news of a new life and an inheritance that is imperishable. This new hope and salvation is made certain or secure through the resurrection of Jesus Christ.

The readers are suffering (1:6) and Peter encourages them in their faith by setting their present suffering into the context of God's overarching purpose.

First impressions
1. Read 1 Peter 1:3-12 carefully and in several different translations if possible. See if you can divide it into three sections. What is spoken to in each part?

a. _____

b. _____

c. _____

2. What is the most important thought in this passage for you?

_____

_____

3. What do you find hard to understand?

_____

The new birth

The apostle addresses the hearers as persons who have been born again, or reborn to a new and different life. The idea of a second birth is well represented in the New Testament and in the early church even though the Greek word *anagennaó* (born anew) is used only in 1 Peter 1:3 and 1:20 in the New Testament.

The rebirth of a person happens through the *mercy* of God and by his will and action (John 1:3; James 1:18), not by human action. Peter says we are reborn to a new and living hope and to an eternal inheritance (1:3). To be reborn is to take part in a new righteousness (1 John 2:29; 3:9; 1 Peter 1:13f.) love (1 John 4:7) and a new victory over the world (1 John 5:4).

The new birth is one of the many ways that the Scriptures speak about salvation. Other words that are used are:

1. *Justified* (the language of the courts)
2. *Redeemed* (the language of the slave market)
3. *Reconciled* (the language of peacemaking)
4. *Propitiation* (the language of the sacrificial system)

All give us part of the meaning of salvation. It is this salvation Peter is speaking about.

The resurrection

What has the resurrection to do with this new hope? It

_____

_____

Born to a new life (1:3-5)

1. Notice that the first paragraph of the body of the letter begins with a doxology (or praise song)—"Praise be to God" (1:3). What does this tell us about the writer's attitude?

_____

_____

_____

2. How does this doxology tie in with what follows immediately in the next sentence? Why does he praise God (1:3)?

_____

_____

_____

3. How is mercy expressed by God? What have we received as a result of his great mercy (1:3)?

_____

_____

_____

4. Through what action has God given us this new hope (1:3)?

_____

5. Not only have we been born anew into a new hope

and a new life but also into an _____

_____ that can never perish (1:4).

guarantees or assures the hope. Notice how during the earthly ministry of Jesus there were two different opinions of his work. The disciples and those who believed took him to be the Christ, the Messiah (Mark 8:29), but the scribes from Jerusalem said he was serving Satan, the prince of demons (Mark 3:22). Both claimed to speak for God. Each believed he was right.

When Jesus was crucified it almost seemed as if the scribes had been right. Yet, when God raised Jesus from the dead, everything became clear. The disciples knew that he was both Lord and Christ (Messiah) (Acts 2:36). From that time on, the resurrection was the living proof that Christ had overcome sin and death and that we too should live in him as he himself said (1 Cor. 15:20-21; John 11:25-26).

The inheritance

In the Old Testament, the inheritance of God meant Israel, the people, Mount Zion and the temple. But more often inheritance had to do with who would receive the father's property and this was governed by law (Deut. 21:15-17). Important to Israel was the promise that the land of Canaan was the inheritance of Israel (Deut. 4:21; 19:14). It was even stated in the Lord's words to Joshua: "You will lead these people to inherit the land I swore to their forefathers to give them" (Josh. 1:6). It was confirmed later by the prophets. Jeremiah sees it as "the most beautiful inheritance of any nation" (Jer. 3:19).

The New Testament also speaks about the son inheriting the possessions of the father (Matt. 21:38) but most often the term is used in a spiritual, symbolic or theological sense. Eternal life can be inherited (Luke 18:18) through the grace of God (Acts 20:32) and the Holy Spirit is a guarantee of this inheritance (Eph. 1:18). It is seen at times as a reward for obedience (Col. 3:24) or as received through the righteousness of faith (Rom. 4:13) but it will not be inherited by the immoral (1 Cor. 6:9-10).

6. What words are used to describe this inheritance?

_____

What do these words want to point out (1:4)?

_____

_____

_____

7. How is the word "inheritance" used in the following passages?

Exodus 15:17 _____

Mark 12:7 _____

Acts 7:5 _____

Acts 20:32 _____

Hebrews 9:15 _____

8. What guarantees the inheritance? How does the writer tie the Christian's faith to the sustaining power of God (1:5)?

_____

_____

_____

9. Peter speaks of a salvation that is "ready to be revealed in the last time" (1:5). Is this the same as the salvation already experienced in the new birth (1:3) or is it different?

_____

_____

_____

10. Notice that 1:20 and 4:7 also refer to the "last time." What might the writer have had in mind (1:5)?

_____

Peter uses the word *inheritance* as the goal of the new birth.

Salvation

Peter speaks of a salvation that is "ready to be revealed in the last time" (1:5). He speaks of a *future* salvation after having spoken about having already been born again to a new hope (1:3). How are these two statements related?

We usually speak about salvation as having occurred in the past at the time when we were born again, that is, when we first believed. But the Bible speaks of salvation as happening in the past, present, and future. It speaks of "having been saved" of "being saved" and about the fact that we "will be saved." All three are true at the same time. Paul also speaks about the past salvation (Eph. 1:13), the present (Phil. 2:12), and the future (Rom. 13:11; Phil 1:19). So, we can say, "I have been saved," and, to express the confident hope, we can say, "I will be saved."

Peter reminds the Christians of three dimensions to salvation. They have already been born anew to a living hope and have been saved from sin. Now they are called to sanctification and holiness which is a process of being saved from sin. And, finally, he points them to the future when this salvation shall be revealed in its fullness.

The persecution

The Christians in Asia Minor were experiencing a good bit of suffering. Why they were suffering is mentioned only indirectly. From the apostle's words, we can guess that they were suffering because of their new lifestyle and their new life in Christ.

When did this persecution take place? There were three main periods of persecution under the Roman emperors: 1) during the time of Trajan who reigned from A.D. 98-117; 2) during the time of Domitian (A.D. 81-96);

_____

_____

A variety of trials (testings) (1:6-9)

The Christian's new life has to be lived out in the real
world. In each period in history and in each place, the
ways of life are a little different. The situation the apostle addresses here is one of suffering. We are not told the
details of how and why the Christians suffered but they
are placed into the context of the Christians' salvation
for all time and compared with the short time of suffering.

1. To what do the opening words "In this" (1:6) refer?
Try to express it by completing this sentence:

"Because you _____

_____ you

greatly rejoice."

2. The trials or testings were real to the people and
could not be treated as insignificant. But what does the
writer do to put them into another light (1:6)?

_____

_____

3. What contrast does the apostle set up between final
salvation (1:5) and the present trials (1:6)?

_____

_____

4. The apostle sees these testings as being a) for a little while, b) varied, and c) as necessary. What purpose
might these testings serve in the Christian's life?

_____

_____

and 3) during the time of Nero (A.D. 54-68). All of these assume, however, that the sufferings mentioned in the letter were caused by official government action against Christians. The letter gives little evidence that government action was involved. What is referred to is that Christians were suffering at the hands of fellow citizens. The Christians' walk or conduct was such that it challenged the values and customs of the society. They were suffering because they chose to follow Christ and let it be known through their deeds.

Because Christians were suffering for doing good, Peter feels the need to comfort them and to encourage them in their walk and witness. He encourages them by indicating that they may actually have been called by God to suffer (2:21).

The word of the prophets

The prophets spoke of things to come but their message is not to be confused with fortune-telling, soothsaying, or magic of some kind. They spoke of the future on the basis of the covenant that God had made with his people (John 7:21-23). If the people would be obedient to the will of God (expressed in the law of the covenant), they would be blessed by God; if they were disobedient to the covenant, they would be punished for their disobedience. Thus it was not difficult for the prophets to announce the coming judgment of God when they saw their people openly disobeying the covenant (Amos 5:21-27).

On the other hand, the prophets had seen in God's dealing with the people that God was a faithful God and fulfilled the divine promises to the people even though they proved unfaithful. On this basis, they could announce that God would lead them out of their Exile and back to the Promised Land (Isa. 40:3), make a new covenant with them (Jer. 31:31f; Heb. 8:1-13), and take upon himself the sin of the people (Isa. 53).

When the prophet announced the coming salvation

5. Have you ever thought of suffering as being necessary? Could this change our attitude to suffering?

_____

_____

_____

6. Can one rejoice in one's salvation while suffering? What kind of rejoicing is it? Compare Matthew 5:11-12 and Colossians 1:24.

_____

_____

_____

7. In what way does suffering prove your faith? Would you know the depth of your faith if it were never put to the test? How?

_____

_____

_____

8. What does the writer foresee as the final outcome of such testing (1:7)?

_____

_____

_____

9. Does loving Jesus depend on seeing him? If not, are those who saw the Lord no more privileged than the rest? (See John 20:29.)

_____

_____

_____

through God's suffering servant or king, they knew that they were speaking to future events. What they did not know was precisely how and through whom God would fulfill their word.

Proof of the prophetic word (1:10-12)

These verses confirm the salvation that was promised by the prophets of Israel.

1. In what way did the prophets of earlier years (e.g., Isa. 7:14) already speak of the salvation made known in Christ (1:10)?

---

2. Why did the prophets search out the meaning of their own prophesies? What things did they search for in their own writings (1:10-11)? What did they want to know?

---

3. Who inspired the word of the prophet (1:11)?

---

4. It was revealed to the prophets that they were serving a future generation (1:12). What value might these prophesies have had for the people in the prophet's own day?

---

5. Fill in additional material on the chart of 1 Peter 1:3-12.

A New and Living Hope (1 Peter 1:3-12)

1:3

1:6

1:10

1:12

Born to a new life
Doxology of hope
- by the mercy of God
- born anew
- through the resurrection
Inheritance/Salvation•
Security of hope

Testing of faith
Rejoicing in hope
Presence of suffering
Purpose of the testing
Oriented to the end
Love without having seen

Prophetic confirmation
Prophets predicted salvation
Enquired when? by whom?
Salvation revealed through
    preaching
Prophets served us
Angels

Comments, additions:

Session 3. Holy in all you do

1 Peter 1:13-21

A good foundation for exhortation (encouragement) has been given in the section just studied (1:3-12). The apostle has told his friends that they have been born again to a living, eternal hope; to a salvation that will be revealed fully in the future but which even now is a certainty through the resurrection of Jesus Christ in whom they have placed their trust. On this basis, he encourages them to live a holy life in all their conduct.

First impressions
1. What is the significance of beginning this new section of the letter with a "therefore"? How does it tie in with what has gone before?

_____

_____

_____

2. How much does this "therefore" cover? The immediate verses 1:13-21? or a longer portion 1:13-25? 1:13—2:3? or 1:13—4:10?

_____

_____

3. Why does the apostle exhort them to holy living? In what way does the paragraph before this one (1:3-12) give the basis for the Christian's walk. List reasons.

A review

We have now gotten into the letter and need to reflect on what we have heard the apostle say.

He has told us that salvation is of God the Father, Son, and Holy Spirit. The Father has chosen or elected us, the Spirit has sanctified us and the son has saved us through his death on the cross (1:2).

He made us aware also of the fact that our salvation has a future meaning: a hope and an inheritance (1:3-5). This hope is not diminished or taken away by any trials we may experience here and now (1:6-7) but is secured by faith (1:8-9), and confirmed by the prophetic word (1:10-12).

On this basis, the apostle now exhorts us to holy living (1:13-21). We are to live out what we have become through the new birth, in good conduct. We are to be Godlike in our lives.

Be holy!

The word "holy" is used 229 times in the New Testament. It is used most often of the Holy Spirit but also refers to being holy in our conduct. It is obviously a key word.

In the Old Testament, holiness is spoken of in relation to places, things, seasons, and official persons. The root meaning is that of separation—the separation of the sa-

_____

_____

_____

4. How are belief and action related? How are our doctrinal confessions (which are expressions of our faith) related to our actions (which are also expressions of our faith)?

_____

_____

5. How is what God has done (1:3) related to what we are to do (1:13)?

_____

_____

6. What is the threefold encouragement given in 1:13?

a. _____

b. _____

c. _____

7. "Gird up the loins of your mind" is the traditional translation for the first exhortation. (See Revised Standard Version or King James Version.) Compare this with 1 Kings 18:46 (RSV). What does the writer want to emphasize with this image?

_____

cred from the profane. Thus, if vessels were set apart for service in the temple they were declared holy and should not be "profaned" (Ezek. 20:9, 14, 22; 22:8). The same applies to the priests who were consecrated for service in the temple (Lev. 21:9-12; 22:2, 31-33). They are holy because they have been consecrated in the service of God who is holy.

Holy is what God is. God's life is holy life (Deut. 32:40). God consecrates and makes holy. God made holy the Sabbath (Gen. 2:3) and the temple (1 Kings 9:1-3). God ordains holy commandments, appoints holy priests to perform God's holy will. All these God makes holy by separating them from the profane and making them fully dedicated to God's service.

When God calls a people (or a person), God separates them from their former life in the world and asks them to do God's will. As they become obedient, they become separated (nonconformed to) from the world and become God's own peculiar people (2:9). Thus the Christians are the "called out ones" (*ekklesia* is the Greek word), which is what the word "church" means. When we exhort someone, we call them out of the life they now live and ask them to live a life more in harmony with the character of God. The word *exhort* has the same root meaning as the word *church*. When Paul addressed the churches he called them holy ones or saints (Col. 1:4) because they had received the spirit of Christ.

You were redeemed

In Greek society generally, the word for "redeemed" was used for the ransoming of prisoners of war, the freeing of a slave, or the buying of pledges. A specific sum of money was paid in each case.

In the Greek Old Testament (the Septuagint) this word is used for the redemption of the firstborn or the firstfruits of every womb (Exod. 13:11-13). This was done to remind the people of Israel that God had redeemed

8. How does "be sober" (RSV) differ from "be self-controlled" (NIV)?

9. Why is strenuous, sober thinking needed for those who live the Christian life?

10. Why is it important to fix your hope firmly on the grace to be revealed in the future?

11. If suffering was a distraction for first-century Christians and they needed to be encouraged to fix their hope on the salvation to be revealed, what are the things that distract us today from living truly Christian lives?

New birth and new life (1:14-16)
Through the mercy of God, they have been born anew to a living hope. Therefore, they are to live lives that reflect this new relationship to God. They are to be holy even as God who called them is holy.
1. As Christians become obedient to Christ, what will happen? How will they relate to their former life (1:14)?

them from a life of slavery in Egypt (Exod. 13:14-16). The prophets later speak of the redemption out of Exile (Zech. 10:8) as does Luke in the New Testament (Luke 1:68).

Redemption carries a price tag. But Peter says that no monetary value can be set for our redemption. We have not been redeemed with silver and gold, the way a slave was redeemed, but with a life. Christ gave his life to redeem us (Mark 10:45). Nothing less than Christ's death could buy us back. This ought to move us to live no longer to ourselves but to him who died for us (2 Cor. 5:15).

Redeemed through the blood of Christ

God made a covenant with his people and the people promised to do all that the Lord commanded (Exod. 19:8). In the following days and years, however, they did not always remain obedient to their promise. They broke the covenant through their disobedience. God, however, provided for their salvation through the medium of the sacrifice.

Though there were many different sacrifices, each for a specific purpose, the meaning of the sacrifice is clear. The worshiper (sinner) brings a pure and spotless lamb to the altar. The worshiper then identifies him or herself with the perfect lamb and presents it fully or wholly to God. The life of the lamb, represented by the blood, is offered to God by being dashed against the foot of the altar. The worshiper in this way declares that he or she offers himself or herself totally to God in the way the lamb has been offered. When this was done in all sincerity, the sin was covered.

The New Testament writers use this image when speaking about the death of Christ. Jesus lived in perfect obedience to the will of God (Heb. 9:28) and as a result was crucified. He gave his life, his blood, himself perfectly to God. Through his obedience and death he

_____

_____

_____

2. Will everything in their former life be seen as evil? In what sense could the answer be yes and in what sense could the answer be no?

_____

_____

_____

3. When was the time that they "lived in ignorance" (1:14)?

_____

_____

_____

4. What positive action will result from the Christians' obedience to Christ (1:15)? How are obedience, Christlikeness, and holiness linked together?

_____

_____

_____

5. What does it mean to "be holy as God is holy" (Lev. 11:44)? (See the note on "Be Holy" on p. 27.)

_____

_____

_____

6. Notice the emphasis on obedience, nonconformity, and holiness in 1:14-16.

Drawn to holy living (1:17-21)

The apostle has already shown that God's holiness

opened up the possibility of our redemption. If we now stand with Jesus, our sin is forgiven and we are born to a new and living hope. It is through him that we believe in God (1:21).

makes us want to be holy also. Other reasons for living clean lives are given in 1:17-21.

1. How does the fact that God is holy encourage us (1:15-16)?

_____

_____

2. How does the fact that God is an impartial judge move us to good conduct as Christians in an unfriendly society (1:17)?

_____

_____

3. Peter reminds us that it cost Jesus his life to redeem us and to give us new life (1:18-19). How does this help us to live a holy and obedient life?

_____

_____

4. In what way was the earlier life "handed down to you from your forefathers" empty? Does that apply as well to us today (1:18)?

_____

_____

5. Jesus, we are told, was foreordained to accomplish our salvation. This was set even before creation! How does this move us to good conduct (1:20)?

_____

_____

Signs of the New Life (1 Peter 1:13–2:10)
Called to Holy Living (1 Peter 1:13-21)

1:13

1:14 Call to Holiness

1:17 Incentives

1:21

Introduction

Because -
Therefore
Be sober
Gird up your mind
Set your hope on grace

Obedience
Nonconformity
Reverent living
Conquering passions/former life
Confidence in Christ

Grace of God
Character of God
Impartial judgment of God
Price of your redemption

Comments, additions:

6. The one who chose Jesus for our salvation (1:20) is also the one who raised Jesus from the dead and the one through whom we have been born anew to a living hope (1:3). What assurance does that give us? How will it further move us to live our lives?

_____

_____

_____

What does this say to us?

It is so easy for us to read these encouragements as being spoken to people in the first century. But they also apply to us. It is not always easy to say exactly how they apply to us in detail. It will be helpful to spend a few minutes on some possible applications of these teachings to our own lives.

1. Write out what God has done for you? Use your own words to express your faith.

_____

_____

_____

2. Now add the "therefore" of verse 1:13. Therefore what? What kind of life does your confession of faith call for?

_____

_____

_____

3. Suppose you are writing to some persons who have recently become Christians and have left their former life of "ignorance," what would you encourage them to do?

Session notes

_____

_____

_____

_____

_____

_____

_____

_____

_____

_____

_____

_____

_____

_____

_____

_____

_____

_____

_____

_____

_____

_____

_____

_____

_____

_____

_____

_____

4. What could you tell young persons today to make them want to live clean lives?

_____

_____

What would you say to adults? _____

_____

5. Would your encouragement to holy living say something about riches/poverty or war/peace, for example? Would it include social action?

_____

_____

_____

6. Record your own observations on 1 Peter 1:13-21 on the diagram for this passage on page 35.

Session notes

_____

_____

_____

_____

_____

_____

_____

_____

_____

_____

_____

_____

_____

_____

_____

_____

_____

_____

_____

_____

_____

_____

_____

_____

_____

_____

Session 4. Grow up in your salvation

1 Peter 1:22—2:3

The life to which Christians are called includes holiness (1:14-16), love to one another (1:22-25), and Christian growth (2:1-3). We took note of the call to holiness in the previous lesson. The call to love is tied closely to the call to holiness. Just as God is holy (1:16), so God is also love (1 John 4:16).

Our newfound hope in God leads to an inner cleansing (1 John 3:3) and makes real love for others possible.

The call to love is not the same as it was for some of the Jews, a call to the outer observance of rules, but a call to love one another from the heart (1:22). We love one another because God first loved us (1 John 4:10, 19). To love one another in John's view is to witness to the world that God is love. All the world will come to know that "you are my disciples if you love one another" (John 13:35).

Love one another (1:22-25)
1. How does the writer link what he says about love with the encouragement he began in 1:14? What is the common element?

_____

_____

_____

Purified! (1:22)

The word for purify (*hagnizo*) is used only six times in the New Testament. In John 11:55, it refers to the purification ritual associated with preparation for Passover. Acts 21:24, 26 refer to Paul joining four other men in a rite of purification. These were external ceremonial rites enjoined by the law (Exod. 19:10-15). In James 4:8, 1 John 3:3, and 1 Peter 1:22, the word refers to the inner purification of which the outer is a symbol.

Purity relates to God just as holiness does. The process of becoming holy as God is holy is known as sanctification (1 Cor. 6:11; Eph. 5:26). The process, when seen in terms of purity, is known as purification (1 Pet. 1:22).

Purification through obedience

The apostle assumes both (1) that the Christians have been obedient and (2) that they have been purified through their obedience. This raises the question: How does obedience purify or cleanse us?

We talked earlier about God calling people out of the world and making them his own peculiar people. Purification refers to the same basic process. God comes to us where we are in society and at whatever level of Christian growth he finds us to be in. Not all of our life is pure and holy, nor do we always do what would be the right

2. How does obedience to the truth purify or cleanse us (1:22)?

_____

_____

_____

3. How is obedience to the truth tied to "love one another" (1:22)?

_____

_____

_____

4. Notice once again the references to the new birth in 1:3 and 1:23. In 1:3 we were born anew "through _____

_____ "

and here we have been born again "through _____

_____ of God." Do these passages say the same thing? How can they be brought into agreement with each other?

_____

_____

_____

5. Read 1 John 2:3-6. How are obedience and knowing God related?

_____

_____

How do we know we are of God or born again?

_____

_____

6. How is the new birth linked to love for one another? Look up 1 John 3:10 and 4:10-21 for a suggested answer.

thing. But God comes to us with his word of promise and reveals to us what we should do. God leads us through his Spirit to know what we could do that would represent the next stage of growth both in spirit and in deed. As we are obedient to this new knowledge of God's will, we are purified, that is, we become more Christlike.

For example, I may have been quite happy with the way I lived with my neighbors. When they bothered me, I ignored them. When they provoked me, I tried not to be unkind. But then the Spirit reminded me through the Word that I should do good to them in spite of such provocation. Obedience to this new demand could well turn the whole thing around. What is more important is that obedience would lead to my spiritual growth.

"Brotherly(?) love"

The New Testament uses the term "brotherly love" (*philadelphia*) six times. Originally the term was used to describe the love between brothers and sisters in a family. Here it is used to mean the love of one Christian for another. (Cf. Rom. 12:10; 1 Thess. 4:9; Heb. 13:1.) Jesus called everyone who believed in him and who followed him "brother," "sister," or "mother" (Mark 3:35; Matt. 12:50). Later the church began to use "brotherly love" and "brotherhood" (1 Pet. 1:22; 5:9) to mean the whole Christian community. In that day, most people felt it was all right to speak this way. When we use such words today, women feel left out. We need to find ways of speaking that do not offend and that include everyone, women and men.

The word

At various points in this letter, the apostle refers directly to passages in the Old Testament. The word is received as truth. It is used to support whatever point is being made in the writing. It suggests that the Scriptures were

_____

_____

_____

7. How does the writer bring together the imperishable and enduring word with the new birth? How are the Scriptures related to faith and the new birth (1:23)?

_____

_____

_____

8. Look up 1 John 3:9. What does the new birth do for our Christian walk?

_____

_____

_____

9. Does the quotation from Isaiah 40:6-8 (used in 1:24-25) apply to the new birth or the Scriptures?

_____

_____

_____

10. What is the main point of this quote from Isaiah in 1:24-25?

_____

_____

_____

11. The apostle says, "This is the Word that was preached to you." What does "this" refer to? What word of Jesus does it remind you of? Matthew 5:17-18?

_____

_____

accepted as the word of God and as authoritative. Is this still the case today?

If you observe what we as Christians say and do, you will often find an inconsistency in some of our responses. Sometimes we will say loudly that we accept the authority of the Scriptures, but then we let our actions be guided by more practical standards. At other times, we hold Scripture to be authoritative but then interpret Scripture in such a way as to make it say what we would like it to say. How can we truly place ourselves under the word rather than making ourselves masters of the word?

Obedience and baptism

Some writers suggest that since obedience refers to a concrete act of obedience, the apostle probably had in mind their obedience to the word in baptism. This is a distinct possibility in that obedience in baptism would not be different from obedience to Christ's bidding in other areas.

It would be advisable, however, to see obedience as an ongoing response to the prompting of the Spirit. The Spirit leads us from truth to truth. If we are obedient in the first thing, the Spirit can lead us to deeper things. In this way, we should be able to constantly grow in sensitivity, applying the gospel to new situations.

12. Do you feel you have real love for your brothers and sisters in the faith? Where do you feel you need more grace? _____

_____

13. Is a greater love for each other needed in your congregation? What genuine signs of love do you observe? _

_____

_____

14. What are some areas of tension or lovelessness that need to be overcome?

_____

_____

_____

_____

Grow as Christians (2:1-3)

The mention of the Word proclaimed to the church (1:24-25) reminds the apostle of the many commands for holy living given in Scripture. He knows that it is as the Word lives in them that they are able to overcome sin and evil (1 John 2:14). A close correlation is seen between *knowing* the word and will of God, *obedience* to the will of God and Christian growth. There is no such a thing as a spiritual plateau. Either we grow in faith and sensitivity to good and evil or we lose our sensitivity to the things of God. We cannot stand still. We are called upon to exercise our faculties to distinguish right from wrong (Heb. 5:14). We are to do so by feasting on the Word.

1. To what does the "therefore" in 2:1 refer? Does it apply to what immediately comes before it or to the larger context?

Called to Love and Growth (1 Peter 1:22—2:3)

1:22   1:25   2:3

1:22 Called to Love

Assumption: New life of holiness
  obedience to the truth
Exhortation: Love one another
Made possible by the new birth
  by the word of God
Confirmed by the prophetic word

Comments, additions:

2:1 Called to Growth

Assumption: New life of holiness
  obedience to the truth
  confirmation of the prophetic word
Exhortation:
Put away all sin (malice), deceit,
  hypocrisy, envy, slander
Long for the pure milk of the word

_____

_____

2. Is 1 Peter 2:1 a general encouragement or were the Christians here in danger of these particular vices?

_____

_____

3. What sins are mentioned? List them.

_____   _____

_____   _____

4. Are these sins a problem for us today? What particular form can they take?

_____

_____

5. What would the catalog of vices look like if written to the church today? Take a moment to list some that you would include.

_____   _____

_____   _____

_____   _____

6. Does 2:2 suggest that the hearers were still babes in Christ? Why? Why not?

_____

_____

7. How are they to relate to the Word (1:2)?

_____

8. Some translate "spiritual milk" as the "milk of the Word." Does this change the meaning of the verse? Does it make it more specific? In what way?

9. How does "knowledge of the Word" aid Christian growth? What is your experience?

10. How does having "tasted that the Lord is good" (2:3) help to get "rid . . . of malice" (2:1) and to grow in salvation (2:2)?

11. How does all of this help us to obey as mentioned in 1:14 and 1:22?

12. How would you tell new Christians to grow in their faith? What practical suggestions could you make?

13. What has been most helpful to you in your Christian growth?

_____

_____

_____

14. Do the things that have been helpful to you appear in your advice to others? If not, why not?

_____

_____

_____

15. What would you suggest for the growth of those who have been Christians for many years and have perhaps lost the freshness of their faith?

_____

_____

_____

16. What might the apostle mean by "growing up in your salvation" (2:3)?

_____

_____

17. What does having "tasted that the Lord is good" mean?

_____

_____

_____

18. Write out the thoughts you wish to remember on the outline sheet on page 47.

Session notes

_____

_____

_____

_____

_____

_____

_____

_____

_____

_____

_____

_____

_____

_____

_____

_____

_____

_____

_____

_____

_____

_____

_____

_____

_____

_____

_____

Session 5. Living stones in a spiritual house

1 Peter 2:4-10

Till now the apostle has been speaking to all the Christians: their new life in Christ (1:3-12); their call to holiness (1:13-21), love (1:22-25), and Christian growth through the knowledge of the word (2:1-3). Now he turns to the Christians and urges them to be the body of Christ in the world (2:4-10). To the degree that Christ will be seen in the church, they will be a "royal priesthood" in the world—that is, they will be his witnesses to the world (Acts 1:8).

The call to be built up in him as a spiritual house is supported by three Scripture references relating to the stone rejected by the builders but chosen to be the chief cornerstone. It is not only a reference to the words of the Prophet Isaiah (8:14; 28:16) and the psalmist (118:22) but to these words of the prophets as interpreted by Jesus. Jesus used these verses to interpret the parable of the unfaithful tenants (Matt. 21:42; Luke 20:17). He pointed to the church which should become the new people of God.

1. Read the parable of the tenants (Matt. 21:33-43) and note how Jesus uses Psalm 118:22-23 to interpret the meaning of the parable. What does Jesus say about the parable?

_____

_____

Stone and cornerstone

Jesus applied the reference to the chief cornerstone in Psalm 118:22 to himself (Mark 12:10, Matt. 21:42 and Luke 20:17). Earlier the Israelites had taken this stone to be the top stone or "coping stone" as referring to Israel. Peter in his sermon to the Jews in the court at Jerusalem leaves no doubt but that it referred to Jesus (Acts 4:11-12) as the one and only Savior. (See Eph. 2:20.)

The reference to the cornerstone in Isaiah 28:16 does not refer to the coping stone but to part of the foundation of the cornerstone. But in the New Testament, Jesus is also seen as the foundation (1 Cor. 3:11). This seems to be the meaning in this passage in 1 Peter. Christ is the cornerstone of the church. So Christ is both the foundation of the church and the head of the church. (See Col. 1:17.)

Christ is described as the living stone. As we noted (1:3), he was raised from the dead and the church is even now built up in him as a spiritual people.

A chosen people

Exodus 19:5-6 described how Israel became a chosen people. God entered into a covenant with them. This was a special relationship in which God promised to be their God and the people promised to do God's will—to keep God's commandments. They were to be the instrument

2. The phrase "as you come to him" in 2:4 is often translated as a command: "Come to him" (RSV). To whom are we to come? Who is implied by this name (2:4)?

3. What is said about this person in 2:4?

4. What does the writer have in mind in speaking about the living stone? (Check one.)

_____ a. The parable told by Jesus?

_____ b. The fulfillment of this word of Jesus in his own death and resurrection which also called into being the church?

5. How did Jesus become the chief cornerstone?

6. What do the following words mean when applied to Jesus (4:7)?

a. *Living* Stone _____

b. *Rejected* Stone _____

c. *Chosen* Stone _____

d. *Precious* Stone _____

7. Read 2:4-5 leaving out the phrase "rejected by men but chosen by God and precious to him." What do the verses say? What will happen?

through whom God's name would be made known among the nations.

From this, it is evident that Christians now stand in a special relationship to God as chosen; that they are to be obedient to God's will and that they are to be God's servants and witnesses.

A royal priesthood
In the old covenant, the priests had access to the courts of the priests and to the holy place in the temple, but only the high priest could enter the most holy place and that only on the day of the atonement (Heb. 9:6ff). It symbolized that the people did not have access to God since God was represented as dwelling in the most holy place (Heb. 9:8).

When Christ was crucified the veil between the holy place and the most holy place was torn open and it symbolized that now, through Christ, all had access to God. This is in harmony with the teaching of the apostle Peter who indicates that all the believers belong to this holy priesthood (2:9) and are called to offer up spiritual sacrifices (2:5).

A holy nation (people)
We are called to be holy even as God is holy. (See notes on 1:15-16.) In that sense, we are to be a holy people or nation. The word for "nation" is *ethnos* and can mean "Gentiles" or "pagans" as in 1 Peter 2:12 and 4:3 (cf. RSV and NIV) or it can refer to a "people" as in this instance.

A people belonging to God
The King James Version reads "a peculiar people" (1 Pet. 2:9). This would be a good translation were it not for the fact that people take "peculiar" to mean "weird." The literal meaning of this Greek word *peripoyesis* is that of "acquiring for oneself." Christians are God's own

8. Now read the same part of 2:4-5 but use the imperative "Come to him, to that living stone . . . and like living stones be yourselves built into a spiritual house." What difference does it make?

_____

_____

_____

9. What does 2:5 imply about all of us being priests?

_____

_____

10. What sacrifices would be acceptable offerings to God (2:5)?

_____

_____

Bible quotes (2:6-8)

1. What do the quotations from Isaiah and Psalms contribute to this appeal? How does the apostle use them to support his message (2:6-8)?

_____

_____

_____

2. Notice again Matthew 21:44 and its negative message. How does the apostle in 2:7-8 distinguish between what the chief stone means for believers and for nonbelievers?

_____

_____

3. Why does the Chief Cornerstone become a stumbling block to some? Why do they reject Christ (2:8)?

_____

people, they are God's own purchased possession (Eph. 1:14). Christians may be very ordinary people but they have value, dignity, and greatness because they belong to God.

A review

We have now begun to understand the direction in which the apostle is taking us. It may help us to cast a look back at the thoughts covered.

The apostle lays a firm foundation for the exhortations he wants to give. He addresses those who have been born again to a new hope, who have received a new life and inheritance through the life of Jesus Christ (1:3-5). He is mindful of the fact that his hearers are suffering for their faith (1:6f.) but know that they love Jesus even though they have not seen him (1:8-9). He encourages the hearers in their faith by pointing out that these things were already spoken of in the prophetic word.

Verse 13 represents a transition. The apostle now exhorts them to holy living on the basis of the hope they have in Christ. Because of what God has done (begotten them anew) they are now to live a holy life. They are called to be holy even as God is holy (1:14-16). The new life in Christ calls for a break with the past, with their former way of life (1:17-18). This is of course not in their own power to do, but they have been set free (purchased their freedom) through the blood of Christ (1:18-19).

Through a life of discipleship (obedience) they are now to manifest genuine love one to another (1:22f). The word of God is to be their sustaining power and to give them that growing edge at all times (2:1-3).

Most important, he calls all of them to come to Christ, the chief cornerstone, and be built up in him as a spiritual house (2:4f). They are to incarnate the life of Christ in the world (2:9-10). They are to be his witnesses, or witnesses *to* him in the world.

We too must recognize ever afresh what God has done

_____

_____

4. Why were they "destined" to stumble? Is it related directly to unbelief and disobedience? How?

_____

5. How does Paul interpret this passage in Romans 9:30-32? Does this help to answer the previous questions?

_____

_____

_____

The witness of the church (2:9-10)
The apostle now returns to describing the nature of the church as a spiritual house, or people. He has made a lengthy digression occasioned by his reference to Jesus as the cornerstone, but now he returns to exhort the believers to be God's own people, declaring the praises of God to all people.

1. Write down all the words used for the church in 2:9. Are any added in 2:10?

_____   _____

_____   _____

2. Where do these descriptions or designations of the church come from? Does your Bible indicate references in the margin or at the bottom of the page? Try Exodus 19:5-6 and Isaiah 43:21 for an answer. Read these passages. What is said in each of them?

Exodus 19:5-6

_____

for *us* (the indicative) this will help us to know what we are to do (the imperative). What God *will do* by way of revealing the fullness of our salvation should also be a motivating factor in our day-to-day choices and decisions.

Isaiah 43:21

3. Why did the apostle describe the church with words that had always been used to describe Israel as the people of God?

_____

_____

4. What do each of these four terms mean?

a. "Elect" or "chosen" race (people) _____

_____

b. Royal priesthood _____

c. A holy nation _____

d. A peculiar people (belonging to God's people) _____

5. Above we noted that the people of God were to offer "spiritual sacrifices." What new tasks are added in 2:9?

_____

6. What is the church to declare to the nations
a. about being called into his wonderful light (2:9)?

_____

b. about being made "a people of God" (2:10)? Look up Hosea 1:8, 10.

_____

c. about "having received mercy" (2:10)? Again look up Hosea 1:8, 10.

_____

7. What would you say is the purpose of the church in the world today?

Called to Become the Body of Christ (1 Peter 2:4-10)

2:4

2:6 Spiritual proof

Isa. 28:16 Cornerstone
Ps. 118:22 Capstone
Isa. 8:14 Stone of stumbling

2:9 People of God

A chosen people
A royal priesthood
A holy nation
A people belonging to God

2:10

Come to him
Come (RSV)
Coming (NIV)
Christ the cornerstone
Living, rejected
Chosen, precious
Church as living stones
Build into a spiritual
house
Offer up sacrifices

Comments, additions:

_____

_____

_____

8. What would be the best witness that the church could make in the world today?

_____

_____

_____

9. The church is called the new humanity. In what way is this a true description?

_____

_____

_____

10. Using the new humanity idea, describe the kind of church you would like to see. What is new?

_____

_____

_____

11. Notice the two diagrams of the letter. The first charts the verses covered in this lesson (2:4-10). The second covers the whole section (1:13—4:10).

a. By the first chart, write two or three important ideas that you want to remember from this lesson (2:4-10).

b. Then think back over Sessions 3—5 and write several truths gained from your study of this whole section (1:3—4:10).

Signs of the New Life (1 Peter 1:13—2:10)

Therefore	Called to Holy Living	Called to Love	Called to Growth	Called to Become the Body of Christ
1:13, 14	1:21	1:22 1:25	2:1 2:3	2:4 2:10

PART III. Slaves, wives, husbands, and all of you
(2:11—3:12)

Session 6. Live as servants of God

1 Peter 2:11-17

The apostle has said that the Christians have been born anew to a living hope (1:3-12) and that they are to demonstrate this new life in all their conduct (1:13—2:10). He has urged them to live holy lives. Avoid deceit, hypocrisy and envy, he said. Grow up in salvation so that people will praise God when they hear about you.

The apostle now turns to the problem of how believers live as Christians in the world. Every society has its customs, norms, and structures. Things are done in specific ways and certain values are assumed. How can Christians live in a world when they do not share its values and cannot do what others expect of them? After a general introduction (2:11-12), the apostle speaks to the Christian as citizen (2:13-17), as slave (2:18-25), and as wife or husband (3:1-7). He closes with a general exhortation to all Christians (3:8-12).

First Words (2:11-12)

Verses 11-12 begin a longer section (2:13—3:12). It is stated in general terms and applies to the whole section.

1. Compare verses 1:13 and 2:11-12. Both introduce a longer section of material. What do they have in common?

A people in bondage

Under the Babylonians, the people of Judah, the Southern Kingdom, went into captivity. Here they returned to the Law of Moses and set the synagogue (their school) so that they could hold on to their faith. When Cyrus, the Persian, overthrew the Babylonians, the Jews were allowed to return to Jerusalem. They rebuilt the temple, restored the city wall, and lived once again in the land. Things went well for them under Alexander the Great (ca. 333 B.C.) and under the Ptolemies of Egypt (300 B.C.), but always they remained a people in bondage.

When the Seleucids (from Syria) became their overlords, things began to change. They were taxed more heavily and Antiochus Epiphanes IV forbade the practice of the Laws of Moses and the worship of God in the temple. This led to a Jewish revolt and finally to independence (164-63 B.C.). They cherished their own rule even though it was marked by internal strife, which gave rise to separate sects like the Pharisess and Sadducees.

Under the rule of the Romans (beginning in 63 B.C.), the Jewish people once more resented being under the heel of a foreign power, even though the Romans allowed them extensive self-government under Herod the Great. They longed for the time when they would be free once more.

2. Why would the author begin with a new address like "Dear friends" in 2:11?

3. Why would the apostle once again call attention to the fact that they are "aliens" (exiles) and "strangers" in the world? What makes it proper to speak in this way (2:11)?

4. How do the earlier references to strangers (1:1), to suffering (1:6), and to the cost of redemption (1:18-19) prepare us for this section?

5. What does the writer urge the Christians to do (2:11)?

6. Is this a general exhortation and therefore applicable to all times and settings? If yes, why? If no, why not?

7. How should Christians live in a non-Christian world or society (2:11-12)?

8. Why might non-Christians accuse Christians of doing wrong?

Abstain from fleshly lusts

The NIV translates 1 Peter 2:11 as "abstain from sinful desires." This is to be preferred, since "fleshly lusts" (KJV) has all too often been understood as referring only to sexual sins. The list of things included under sins of the flesh are given by Paul in Galatians 5:19-21 and include wrath, idolatry, witchcraft, and hatred. Thus it is clear that flesh does not refer only to the body but rather to human nature apart from God. Therefore, all desires that lead us away from fellowship with Christ or from a holy life are considered fleshly desires.

Accusations!

The early church, because of its beliefs, faced much opposition. But it was often falsely accused. Many untrue charges were brought against its members and they had no good way of defending themselves. Thus Pliny writes to the emperor Trajan (A.D. 112) and accuses the Christians of singing a hymn to "Chrestus" as to a god. They were accused of atheism because they would not worship the gods of the Greeks and the Romans. They were even accused of cannibalism, which was no doubt the result of a misunderstanding of the Lord's Supper.

Visitation

The words "in the day of visitation" may seem strange to you. We do not use them too often in our conversation. Yet, for the Christian, it has a significant history and meaning.

The children of Israel were told from the beginning that God would come to them either with judgment or with blessing. If they kept the Covenant, it would be life to them, but if they disobeyed God's word and will, it would result in judgment and captivity.

The prophets therefore saw the day of visitation as any day or time in which the Lord came to bless or to judge his people. At the same time, they were aware that this

a. In the day of First Peter? _____

_____

b. In our day? _____

_____

9. What is meant by people giving glory to God after seeing the good works of the Christians?

_____

_____

_____

10. What is meant by "the day he visits us" or "the day of visitation" (RSV) in 2:12?

_____

_____

11. How does all of this relate to witnessing in the world? Should we not rather preach the gospel? Why does the writer emphasize the witness we give to Christ through our conduct?

_____

_____

_____

12. Look ahead to 2:13, 2:18, and 3:1. What idea is common to this whole section? _____

_____

13. In the chart on page 70, show the following:
a. Look up the passages and show which stations are addressed in each reference (left-hand column). For example, Colossians 3:18—4:1 addresses wives, husbands; children, parents; slaves, masters. Place a check mark in the column under wives/husbands and so on.

would occur also in a fuller sense at the end of time. It thus has a dual meaning: (1) here and now and (2) at the end of time.

In 1 Peter 2:12, it can also have this dual meaning. It can mean some special event in their lives which would bring home to them the claims of God or it can mean the judgments of God at the end of time.

Subject to Rome?

The advice to obey the emperor comes as a bit of a surprise. The Jewish people as a whole chafed under heavy taxes and the presence of foreign overlords. In particular, the Zealots had since A.D. 6 directly opposed the Roman governors. The Zealot cause was gaining more followers and greater strength during the time of Jesus and Paul. The Zealots advocated nonpayment of taxes, subversion, and open revolt against Rome. They took every opportunity to win the Jewish people to their side.

Even though the Sadducees tried to retain control of the temple and its services by cooperating and negotiating with the Romans, peace became ever more difficult to maintain. By A.D. 68, at the end of the reign of Nero, the Romans moved against Jerusalem. They destroyed the city (A.D. 70) and scattered the people once more.

In this context, it is surprising to hear both Paul (Rom. 13:1) and Peter (1 Pet. 2:13f.) admonish the Christians to be subject to every human institution and to the emperor. It was clearly a different ethic. Christians were not to revolt or undermine the government, but live as Christians in their station as citizens.

Be subject, but how?

Christians didn't quite know how to respond to governments and governors. They could not participate with the Zealot revolutionaries, nor could they avoid the problem.

It was clear to the apostles from the beginning that

b. Note the resulting pattern. How is 1 Peter different from Colossians and Ephesians?

_____

c. Is the order in which these are given in 1 Peter significantly different?

_____

_____

14. Why does the apostle single out our places in life as citizens, slaves, and wives (or husbands)? Can you think of a reason related to the trials and suffering mentioned in 1:6?

_____

_____

	Citizens	State	Wives	Husbands	Children	Parents	Slaves	Masters
Col. 3:18—4:1			✓	✓	✓	✓	✓	✓
Eph. 5:20—6:9								
1 Peter 2:13—3:7								
Rom. 13:1-7								

one could not simply obey the government or other authorities blindly. One had to follow God rather than human lords (Acts 5:9). They also realized that there is no
authority except from God (Rom. 13:1). Government and
order are of God even if every government does things
that are not of God.

The apostle recognized that the state has a ministry
under God. It is to limit evil and encourage the good.
Each government does this to a greater or lesser degree.
To the degree that a government fulfills its God-given
task, it will receive the support and cooperation of the
Christians in the land.

The Christian, however, is also called to freedom (2:16)
and to do what is right (2:15). This means that the Christian is morally responsible as a person. He/she has to
weigh what is good. At times one may have to disobey an
ordinance of the government if that ordinance is judged
to be contrary to the person's calling in Christ. The
Christian recognizes that absolute allegiance belongs
only to Christ.

Where there must be civil disobedience in order to be
obedient to Christ, the Christian regards it as a witness
to his/her Lord.

Human institutions

The apostle tells us to be subject to every human creation, institution, or structure (*ktises*). The Greek word
has the meaning of creation wherever the word is used in
the New Testament (Mark 10:6; Rom. 1:20, 25; 2 Cor.
5:17). First Peter 2:13, therefore, recognizes that we as
humans create governments, organizations, and structures in order to reach the goals we set for ourselves.
This is in obedience to the command of God to subdue
the earth (Gen. 1:28).

We know, however, that once these governments, organizations, and structures (creations) are in place, they

Submit to every authority (2:13-17)

The first specific station that the apostle chose to address is that of Christians as citizens. Paul had similar things to say in Romans 13:1-7. These two stand in sharp contrast to the way in which the state is spoken of in Revelation 13:1-18. You may wish at some other time to compare these three passages more closely.

The apostle is concerned about how Christians relate to human institutions and structures in society. How does the Christian who is a stranger to this world respond to the structures of governments with all their substructures?

What is the Christian's responsibility?

1. To whom should Christians submit themselves?

_____

_____

2. "Submit . . . to every authority" (v. 13). What does this include? Only governors or also the authorities of other human institutions? (See commentary below.)

_____

_____

_____

3. The apostle says to be subject to kings or to those sent by him (2:13-14). It suggests that he could go on to mention still other authorities. Name some of the authorities and institutions in our day to which this might refer: traffic police? public health nurse? teacher?

_____

_____

_____

4. According to 2:14, what is the purpose of government (the state)? How does this principle compare with Romans 7:1-7?

exercise a powerful hold on us and often determine what we do.

These structures are given of God, in the sense that it is impossible to do without them, and yet they can break down and produce evil rather than good. Of each structure, we are to ask whether it allows us to do good or forces us to do evil. If it forces us to do evil, we will need to break with the structures and suffer for it if need be.

Stations in life

The sections in Colossians 3:18-41, Ephesians 5:20—6:4, and 1 Peter 2:11—3:12 were called *Haustafeln* by Luther. He saw them as rules or precepts for the Christian household. In Luther's day such rules were often displayed in inns and in private homes. I disagree with Luther's label because these rules for wives-husbands, children-parents, slaves-masters, and citizens were not intended so much for the household as for all of society. They were given to help Christians know how they should live as Christians in their stations in life.

A station in life is that place in life where a person has a moral obligation to someone else. Thus as a wife, a woman has a responsibility to her husband, and sons or daughters have obligations to their parents. In the same way, one has ethical obligations in one's station as citizen, car driver, or property owner. We are to be Christian in all of our stations.

The stations of 1 Peter

As you have noticed in completing the diagram on page 70, the stations listed in 1 Peter are fewer than in Colossians or Ephesians. Some of the differences are (1) Christians are spoken to as citizens in 1 Peter and in Romans but not in Colossians and Ephesians; (2) children and parents are not addressed in 1 Peter; (3) masters are not addressed in 1 Peter; (4) husbands are addressed but only in one verse; (5) in 1 Peter, it is assumed that the mem-

---

---

5. What is mentioned in Romans that is not spoken to in 1 Peter 2:13-17?

---

6. Does the exhortation to be subject to the state mean that we obey the authorities even when they call on us to do what is wrong?

---

7. Verse 2:15 assumes that the Christian will do what is right and good no matter what the authorities request. It does not see this as an effort to upset the system but rather as a Christian witness to society. When should one obey God rather than human authorities? See Acts 5:29 for one illustration.

---

8. How could "doing good" put to silence the "ignorant talk of foolish men" (2:15)?

---

9. How does the Christian or the Christian community decide when to obey and when to refuse to do what the authorities ask us to do? What process would be helpful to us in making such decisions?

---

bers addressed (except for husbands) are suffering at the hands of non-Christians.

From this it is clear that the apostle's main concern was for those who were suffering unjustly for being Christian in their stations. This applied to them as citizens, slaves, and wives. The order in which these are arranged may also suggest that their greatest problems were experienced as citizens, then slaves, and then as wives.

The new ethic of the Christian citizen

The Christian citizens accepted the state as of God. They had no intention of undermining the government. They only did what was right under God. But they communicated one thing very clearly and that was that Jesus, not the emperor, is Lord. Ultimate allegiance belongs to Christ.

Governors could see this as a threat to their power and authority. They may have felt secure in their power only if no one was allowed to challenge it. But for the Christians, the emperor too was under God and not a god to his subjects. This idea was a direct threat to the state in that the absolute power of the emperor or any governor was called into question.

Why were the Christians persecuted?

It seems to us that no one should be persecuted for doing good, yet it happens. Think of the many places and areas of life in which people today are suffering through no fault of their own.

The persecution mentioned in 1 Peter, however, is open and deliberate. People suffer because their conduct is Christian! But why? What's behind it all?

The Greeks thought of the family as being one small part of a larger family, the state. The state will be what the family is! If you change the nature of the family, you change the nature of the state.

_____

_____

10. What does "live as free men" mean in 2:16?

_____

_____

_____

11. How is a person advised *not* to use one's freedom (2:16)?

_____

_____

12. How does "live as servants of God" (2:16) limit the use of our freedom and the way we submit to the authorities?

_____

_____

_____

13. In verse 2:17 in the King James Version, the word "honor" is used for both "all men" and "the king." (Note how the NIV translates the instruction for "everyone.") Write out how we are to respond to the following.

a. Everyone _____

b. The believers _____

c. God _____

d. The king _____

14. Do these instructions apply to us today? How are our structures of authority different from the time of 1 Peter? Does this change the basic nature of the message? If so, how? If not, why not?

The Christians were bringing new values and new ideas into their families and society. They understood what it meant to be a citizen, slave, or wife differently than did their fellow citizens. These citizens, however, saw a threat in the conduct of the Christians. They felt the Christians were changing the nature of the family and this was seen as equal to sabotage. They believed it would undermine the total society. Therefore, they opposed the values and actions of the Christian community.

_____

_____

_____

Be Christian in Your Stations (1 Peter 2:11–3:12)

2:11

2:17

General teachings

Address: "Beloved"
Circumstances: Aliens, exiles
  spoken of as evildoers
  living in the world.
Exhortation—Abstain from lust
  maintain good conduct
Motivation—witness
  Day of the Lord

Comments, additions:

2:13 As Citizens

Address: (understood—to all)
Circumstances: state-emperor, governors
  objectives of state—promote good/limit evil
  freedom of Christian
  charges against Christians
Motivation—for the Lord's sake
  put to silence ignorant talk.

Session 7. Under the pain of unjust suffering

1 Peter 2:18-25

The apostle next addresses the Christian in his station as a slave. Some of the slaves had accepted Jesus Christ as Lord and Savior and were no doubt anxious to know how they were to conduct their lives as slaves. They could not simply demand their freedom because that was not in their power to ask, since the master had total power over the slaves. Most of the masters likely did not share their faith and would not respond kindly to such requests. The apostle does not expect that Christian slaves will be given their freedom. The slave will have to learn to live *as a Christian* in the station of a slave. The apostle here seeks to be helpful to the Christian slaves as they seek to be holy in their conduct in the station of a slave. Try to put yourself into the shoes of a Christian slave as you work through this passage.

Be subject as slaves (2:18)
1. With what attitude are slaves to subject themselves, to their masters (2:18)?

2. To what kind of masters are they to be subject? to the kind? wicked? all? Name them.

Slavery

Slavery was known not only in Greek and Roman cultures but also in the ancient Near East. There was a difference, however. In ancient biblical times, the slave could acquire some rights. Slaves could own other slaves, and often had the power to conduct business even while they were under a master. In the later Roman period, the slave had no rights at all and it was more difficult for the slaves to work their way to freedom.

In Judaism, permanent slavery was not allowed. An Israelite slave had to be released after seven years. A non-Israelite woman slave became part of the family. A non-Israelite male slave had to be circumcised (i.e., become an Israelite) within the first year or could not be kept any longer.

It is said that in the Roman Empire there may have been as many as 60 million slaves. Slaves were acquired in war, by purchase, by birth, through debt foreclosures, or self-sale or the sale of one's children. Most slaves were either domestic or in public service.

The master had absolute rights over the slave. He had power of life or death over his slaves, and there were no doubt masters who dealt unjustly with their slaves. Most masters however depended on their slaves for medical help, for the education of their children, and to operate

3. The apostle knows that to be Christian as a slave will mean that the slave will have to be ready to suffer at the hands of the master, yet he sees this as good and commendable. What value does the apostle see in such suffering (2:19)?

---

4. Not all suffering has value. What kind of courageous suffering does the apostle hold to be without value (2:20)?

---

5. What kind of suffering does Peter say is approved by God (2:20)?

---

6. To what does the apostle compare the suffering the slave is going to experience as a Christian (2:21)?

---

7. Is this call to suffering at all linked to their witness in the world (2:11-12)?

The example of Christ (2:21-25)
The Christian slave is to find comfort and strength in the knowledge that he or she is not the only one called upon to suffer. Christ himself, in obedience to God, suf-

businesses. They knew that it was to their own advantage not to mistreat their own servants.

The freeing of slaves

Slaves were often set free. In Judaism, it was understood that a slave would be freed after seven years. In Roman society, a slave could be redeemed or freed for a purchase price, or he could buy his own freedom if he could come to sufficient funds. Most often slaves were given their freedom through the last will of the owner, usually as a reward for service. In one way or another, many slaves were being freed—so much so that governments were worried about the consequences of having too many slaves freed in too short a time. Rome therefore took steps to restrict the freeing of slaves.

Called to suffer

The apostle knew full well that if the slave did what was right and good (2:20), he would have to suffer for it, especially under harsh or wicked masters. This was unavoidable. The slave who regarded himself or herself as serving Christ (Col. 3:23, Eph. 6:5-6) would represent a threat to the authority of the master. Such Christian slaves made their own judgments as to when they could or could not obey their masters. Some masters could not tolerate such a challenge to the accepted structures and punished Christian slaves for their disobedience.

Every structure or institution seeks to make itself final and absolute. If then a society and its customs are challenged (as it was by the Christians), it exerts every effort to ward off such a challenge.

The slave/the laborer

We might think it strange that the early church did not speak more openly against slavery. Why did they not condemn it outright? Why speak to how a person can be Christian as a slave?

fered a cruel death on the cross. Jesus' obedience to God and his patient suffering and subjection to the powers that nailed him to the cross are presented here as a forceful example for the slave to follow (2:21).

1. What does the apostle want to convey about Jesus by quoting the words of the Prophet Isaiah (Isa. 53:9 in 2:22)?

_____

_____

_____

2. Did Jesus' sinlessness and obedience to God prevent the people from abusing him? No, it did not! Put yourself into his place when they hurled insults at him. What would have been your response? What did Jesus do (2:23)?

_____

_____

_____

3. What was the purpose of Christ's suffering according to 2:25? What Scripture does it call to mind? Isaiah

53:6 says _____

_____

4. Why did religious leaders oppose Jesus? Check the following verses.

a. John 5:16 _____

b. Mark 3:1-6 _____

c. John 11:45-47 _____

d. John 4:9, 27 _____

5. The above cases show that Jesus broke with the way of doing things in his day. In what way was he also an example to the slave in doing so?

The reason is that slavery too belonged to human structures and order (2:13). To have simply called for the abolition of slavery would be like calling for the abolition today of the station of laborer. It could not be done without first creating new alternate structures.

The slave in Rome could be compared to our "blue collar" and "white collar" vocations. The slave was the teacher, physician, baker, businessman, and laborer. If the master needed an experienced person in some field, he would have a slave trained to do that work. The master was dependent on the slaves just as the factory owner depends on laborers.

By way of comparison, one might even entertain the thought as to whether the laborer today is not more helpless to affect his own lot than was the slave in first-century Rome. Roman senators were afraid that eventually Rome would be run by slaves who had gained their freedom.

Slavery and the church

In the Christian community, slaves, along with women, were treated as morally responsible members. They were regarded as persons in their own right and not as chattel or possessions. To be treated as morally responsible persons meant that they could choose their own faith and were included in all the moral admonitions of the gospel.

Slaves too were free persons (2:16). This meant they had to evaluate for themselves what they considered to be right or wrong and were held accountable for the choices they made.

The slave as witness

It is almost a paradox that precisely at the point where the Christian's life and conduct become a threat to existing institutions, two quite different things happen:

1. The Christian is called upon to suffer; to suffer the

_____

_____

Slavery as a way of life

Every society has a specific order. The economic, educational, social, political, religious, and other structures of
a society are all linked together. It is not possible to
change one part without touching every other part of
society. For example we could not simply remove the station of laborer from society today without upsetting the
whole society. Slavery was such a structure. It was an
important part of the economic, social, political, and
even religious structures of Peter's day.

1. How did persons become slaves?

Numbers 31:9 _____

Exodus 21:4 _____

Genesis 17:27 _____

Exodus 21:3 _____

Leviticus 25:39 _____

2. What was not allowed according to Deuteronomy
24:7?

_____

3. In the New Testament notice that Paul sends Onesi-
mus, the runaway slave, back to Philemon his owner
(Philem. 1-25). Why would he do so?

_____

_____

4. Why did the Christians not simply call for the abolition of the institution of slavery?

_____

_____

consequences of challenging a well-entrenched institution.

2. It is at this point that the Christian is able to give the clearest and most pointed witness to Jesus as Lord. So it was in the life of Jesus (2:21-25) and so it will be in the Christian's life.

Overcoming an evil institution

The Christians did not rebel against the state, nor against the institution of slavery in any direct action. Neither did they see it as to be defended as being the status quo. Rather, they took away its power and strength by recognizing everyone as a brother and sister in Christ and as servants of the same Lord (Col. 3:23—4:1; Eph. 6:7-9). In this way, the institution of slavery was dissolved because (1) the distinction between slave and master no longer existed, or had power, in the church, and (2) an alternative structure was being put into place that would allow the institution to be replaced by another structure in society. In this sense, the Christians affected a revolution in society without being rebels.

The Christian sees no structure or institution as ultimate. All are human creations in a sense (but also God-ordained) and therefore imperfect. Any institution or structure can be changed. This task of bringing a Christian critique to the structures of society is as relevant today as it was when 1 Peter was written.

Jesus and the powers

We have not always seen to what extent Jesus broke with the traditions, customs, and structures of his day. Some of the ways in which he acted counter to expectations are: (1) He broke with some of the standard interpretations of the law as given by the scribes. He would say, "You have heard that it was said . . ." and then counter with "But I say to you. . ." (Matt. 5:21ff). (2) He

5. Suppose you consider a certain structure to be unjust. Can you simply call for it to be disregarded or abolished (e.g., the educational system, the legal structure)?

6. Now put yourself into the shoes of the many people on earth who have to suffer under unjust political, economic, religious, and other systems that they can't change. What would you as a Christian say to them?

7. How does one best respond to unjust structures?

8. How effective was the response of the early church when they obeyed the apostle's call to (1) be subject and simultaneously (2) to do good, not evil?

9. What possibilities do we have today to speak to the structures of society which the early Christians did not have?

spoke in his own name—not only in the name of Moses as did the scribes. He spoke with an authority that challenged the scribes (Mark 2:21). (3) He broke with the fasting tradition of the scribes (Mark 2:18-22). (4) He talked to the Samaritans and to women (John 4:9, 27). (5) He had women followers whereas scribes would not allow this (Luke 8:1f). (5) He regarded Pilate as having received his power from God (John 19:11). (6) He spoke against those of the scribes who were not true to their calling (Matt. 15:7).

To see that Jesus obeyed God even if it meant breaking with the structures of society should encourage us if we are called on to do so by our Lord.

Session notes

Be Christian in Your Stations (1 Peter 2:11—3:12)

2:18   2:25

As Slaves

Circumstances
  harsh masters
  suffering for doing good
Exhortation:
  be subject
  live by the example of Christ

2:21 Example of Christ

Circumstance: He suffered yet
  he committed no sin,
  made no threats, was righteous
He was crucified
Motivation
  sufferers have God's approval
  called to suffer
  example of Christ

Comments, additions:

Session 8. In harmony with one another

1 Peter 3:1-12

Next the apostle speaks to women in their stations as wives. This may not seem significant to us but the lot of the wife in our culture is different from that of the wife in Hebrew and Greco-Roman societies. One has to appreciate the fact that for the first time the wife was a "joint heir of the grace of life" (3:7 RSV) with her husband. Wives were called upon to be personally accountable to Christ in their walk and thus might not be supported in their newfound faith by their non-Christian husbands. The apostle is writing to this new situation. The question is: will the wife be permitted to keep her Christian faith if her husband does not share the same faith? The apostle answers by asking her to be a witness through her conduct—just as he did of the slave.

Wives be submissive (3:1-6)

1. Wives are asked to be submissive to their husbands even in what circumstances (3:1)?

_____

_____

2. Do mixed marriages (Christian/non-Christian) exist in the same way today? What may be different today?

_____

_____

Women

The gospel clearly created a problem for women in the first-century Greco-Roman world. Through the preaching of the gospel, some became Christians and others not. Thus it happened that a wife or husband would accept Christ but the spouse would not. This was no great problem for the husbands, but it was a problem for the wives.

For the husbands it was a problem only if his family was part of a larger family and his father was still the main authority. Outside of this situation, if the husband became a Christian, his whole household—wife, slaves, grandchildren, and servants—became Christians as well. No inner family conflict was created as a result.

For the wife, it was different. In Judaism, as in the Greco-Roman world, the wife had no legal rights. She was either under the power (and legal control) of her father or her husband. At no point could she choose her own faith without breaking with the accepted system. Legally, she was classed with property rather than as a person with rights. For the wife to change her religion when her husband did not was out of the question. Unthinkable! The husband could divorce her but she could not divorce him. Can you imagine what happened when Christian women held on to their faith in Christ even if their husbands did not become Christian?

3. Does "be submissive" mean unquestioned obedience to the husband? Does it mean the same here as in 2:13 and 2:18? If so, why? If not, why not?

_____

_____

_____

4. Would the wife be expected to do what is right even if the husband asked her to do what was wrong?

_____

_____

_____

5. The apostle asks the wife to remain Christian even if her husband is not a Christian. How does this add to the answers to questions 3 and 4?

_____

_____

_____

6. In what way would she be giving a witness through her Christian conduct (3:1-2)?

_____

_____

_____

7. What is given in the text as inappropriate and appropriate adornment of the wife (3:3-5)?

_____

_____

_____

Wives obey

One would have expected everyone in the first century to say "wives be subject to your husbands." What other choice did they have? But when the apostle says "be submissive," it does not mean what it meant to others. Peter assumes that Christian wives will not reject Christ, no matter how much they may have to suffer. With the wife retaining her faith in Jesus, she was already breaking with the structures of society; she was already doing what was unthinkable in that society. Clearly, to be subject to her unbelieving husband did not mean uncritical or blind obedience, because then she would have had to give up her faith in Christ. To be subject to her husband did not mean being untrue to Christ. Whatever being subject meant, it would be an expression of her Christian faith.

Advice to persecuted wives

It is helpful to notice what advice the apostle did not give the persecuted wives. (1) He did not advise them to denounce Christ and accept their husbands' faith; (2) he did not advise them to leave their non-Christian husbands (cf. 1 Cor. 7:12f.) but to continue in the marriage if they were not rejected; (3) he did not tell them to preach to or nag their husbands. What he did tell them was to be Christian (in word and deed) in their station as wives.

Again the writer assumes that the wife will do what is right and will manifest a Christian spirit of love and respect to her husband and household. She will show such pure conduct (2:12) that there will be no occasion for blame. Her Christian walk will be her witness to the faith because in her situation she would not be allowed to witness publicly or with words.

Adornments

Though the domestic women were always veiled when appearing in public, there were free women in the Ro-

8. How does the author support his exhortation by reference to "women of the past" (3:5-6)?

_____

_____

9. This passage obviously does not answer all of the questions raised with respect to the role of women in society and church today. What issues need to be addressed that are not spoken to here?

_____

_____

_____

_____

Husbands be considerate (3:7)

The exhortation to the husbands is brief in comparison. The problem was much greater for Christian wives than it was for husbands. Nevertheless, what is said to the husbands may be as significant in that setting as the word to the wives. The husband too is given a different word than would have been expected in that society.

1. Notice that "in the same way" is used three times in 1 Peter (3:1, 3:7, and 5:5). In two of the references it is linked with the word "submissive." In what way is 3:7 like the other two?

_____

_____

2. In Greek society, husbands were encouraged to "rule" their wives. How are the husbands asked to live as Christians with their wives (3:7)?

_____

man society who were in a class by themselves. They were known as *heterai*. They were often the daughters of royalty that had been conquered and were now the public consorts of political leaders. They were not allowed to marry and have children but they were allowed to own property. Often they were independently wealthy.

These women knew how to adorn themselves. They would wave and dye their hair or would wear wigs. They would wear hairbands, pins, and combs made of ivory or gold, studded with gems.

Since these women were known as free women and Christian citizens, slaves and wives were to live as free persons (2:16), the temptation for the Christian wives was to look to these free women as models for themselves. The apostle speaks against this. They should rather model themselves after the women of old, like Sarah. Their adornment should be the inner adornment of the self.

Husbands

The apostle begins with "likewise" (RSV) or with "in the same way" (NIV) when addressing husbands. They are to live considerately or in knowledge with their wives. They are to manifest a spirit of mutual respect and care to their wives.

Different was the advice that the philosopher-historian Plutarch gave to the men of that day. He told the men to rule over their wives in such a way that they would not become rebellious.

The most telling part of First Peter's counsel to husbands is that husband and wife are seen as joint heirs of the grace of life. It is in perfect harmony with Galatians 3:28: "There is neither Jew nor Greek, slave nor free, male nor female, for you are all one in Christ Jesus."

_____

_____

3. In the Greek, it actually says "husbands live with them in _knowledge_ and give _honor_ to the wife. . . ." How does this change the meaning of the exhortation from the NIV translation?

_____

_____

_____

4. What could be meant by the apostle when he tells husbands to give honor to their wives as to the weaker "vessel" (KJV)?

a. Physical strength? _____

b. Inferior as a person? _____

c. As having less power in society? fewer "rights"? ___

_____

5. How does the statement that husband and wife are really "joint heirs of the grace of life" (RSV) add a new perspective to this admonition?

_____

_____

_____

6. What is needed in our day for wives and husbands to be truly joint heirs of the grace of life (3:7)?

_____

_____

_____

7. What is meant by "that your prayers be not hindered" (KJV)?

Be Christian in Your Stations (1 Peter 2:11–3:12)

3:1

3:7 As Husbands

3:8 All

3:12

As Wives

Circumstances: The husbands
   are not Christian
   wives tempted by freedom
Exhortation: Be subject
   use inner adornment
Motivation: To win husband
   win approval of God
   example of Sarah

Comments, additions:

As Husbands

Circumstances: The husband
   as believer
Exhortation: Dwell in
   knowledge
   give honor to wife
Motivation: Joint heirs
   that prayers be not hindered

All

Exhortations:
   live in harmony
   be sympathetic/love
   tenderness
   humility
   nonresistance

8. How have the structures that determine the relationship between wives and husbands changed (a) from New Testament times to the twentieth century and (b) from your grandparents' day to your day?

9. Why were the structures changed? Do such reasons exist today? Can a call for change be judged as good from a Christian point of view?

All Christians (3:8-12)

These verses complete this section of the letter. It is a general statement directed at all Christians as they are called upon to live in society. It is a good summary of Christian values that should be applied in any and all circumstances in life.

1. "Finally" could be rendered in terms of "to sum up." In what way does this paragraph sum up what has already been said in 2:11—3:7?

2. The author has spoken about possible and likely strife between citizens and governing authorities, slaves and masters, wives and non-Christian husbands. How does life "in harmony with one another" (3:8) speak to these settings? How is it to be achieved?

Be Christian in Your Stations (1 Peter 2:11—3:12)

Beloved (General intro.)	As Citizens	As Slaves	As Wives	As Husbands	All
2:11-12	2:13	2:18	2:25 3:1	3:7 3:8	3:12

3. What other exhortations are made in verse 8?

4. Can you think of instances where Jesus in his ministry exemplified these qualities?

5. In 3:8, the author speaks to Christian attitudes. In 3:9, he speaks to interpersonal relationship. Compare what is said in 3:9 with 2:23. How do both these passages exemplify Jesus' word in Matthew 5:11?

6. Again the apostle emphasizes that Christians are called to suffer (3:9). Compare this with 2:21. Is it really necessary that Christians suffer? Will they not inherit a blessing without suffering?

7. What purpose does the longer quote from Psalm 34:12-16 play? Can you venture a guess why these verses were chosen by the author? What are some of the general principles touched on in these verses?

Session notes

_____

_____

_____

_____

_____

_____

_____

_____

_____

_____

_____

_____

_____

_____

_____

_____

_____

_____

_____

_____

_____

_____

_____

_____

_____

_____

**PART IV. Those who suffer according to God's will
(3:13—4:19)**

Session 9. Saved by the resurrection of Jesus Christ

1 Peter 3:13—4:11

Born anew to a living hope, the Christian lives a new and holy life. Such a person brings new norms and values to everyday living, a fact that may cause strife and tension with the Christian's fellow citizens. If the Christian persists in right living, suffering will be the result. The author of 1 Peter, therefore, gives attention to the suffering Christians. How will Christians deal with this suffering?

1. Verse 3:13 begins with a rhetorical question. The answer to such questions is usually self-evident. What did the writer expect as an answer?

2. Normally, you will not be called upon to suffer for doing what is right but be ready for the exceptions (3:14). Is it a tragedy if you do suffer for doing right? What is the view of the apostle? Compare with Matthew 5:11-12.

3. The apostle encourages them with a quote from Isaiah 8:12. (Notice also the quote from Isa. 8 in 1 Pet. 2:8.) What comfort is it to be told not to "fear what they fear" or "fear their threats"?

Will the righteous suffer?

This is an age-old question. Will God permit the people who do right to suffer? It doesn't seem right. Job found no reason why he should suffer what he did. The disciples ask who sinned, the blind man or his parents, since he was born blind. Jesus simply reminds them of how God might be glorified through the blind man receiving his sight (John 9:1ff).

Normally, as we said, we do not suffer for doing what is right. But human sin and human structures are such that very often the innocent suffer; very often it is precisely the ones who do good who suffer. This is always an open possibility.

Being Christian and suffering

In discussing citizens, slaves, and wives, we noted that as Christians, we may face suffering. To bring Christian values and deeds to bear on our stations in life may cause us to challenge the accepted expectations and standards of our society and to reap the anger of our fellow citizens.

An intern in a hospital in which I worked as an orderly refused to assist a leading physician when the physician started to sew up the lacerated arm of a drunken man without giving him anything for pain. After a heated exchange, the physician gave the patient a local anes-

_____

_____

4. What does the writer mean by "in your hearts set apart (reverence or sanctify) Christ as Lord"? Does it really mean an inner devotional attitude of worship? Does it mean a resolve to obey Christ, come what may? What do you think?

_____

_____

_____

5. When, in situations of conflict, Christians bring other values to the fray, they will face opposition and challenge. What does the writer tell Christians to do when this happens (3:15f.)?

_____

_____

_____

6. When we answer people's questions about our faith, in what way are we doing evangelism?

_____

_____

_____

7. What are Christians to remember when they are challenged by others (3:16)?

_____

_____

_____

8. How can Christians keep their conscience clean (3:16)? Does this mean only in what is being said or is this also a reference to doing?

thetic and the intern stepped up to the table to assist. Later, a nurse said that he was stupid to take such a stand—he might never graduate! The Christian intern simply said, "I have to do what is right." He simply could not do what the physician asked him to do.

We are called upon as Christians to do what is right rather than what is expected in our stations, as parents, teachers, citizens, or laborers. When we do so, it may be that we will suffer for it—we may lose our jobs, we may lose our popularity, we may not be permitted to advance beyond what we are now doing. We should expect at times to suffer for being Christian.

Do not fear their fear

We are often driven to actions that are contrary to our calling in Christ and our confession of him by the pressures of society. It is not easy to swim against the stream. We fear what people will say, what they will do, and what will happen to us if we challenge expected norms and values or if we simply do what we hold to be right.

The apostle's advice is: Do not fear their overt or implicit threats. Rather, let them fear (reverence) the Lord. He is the one who has the power of life and death.

Be prepared to answer

The wonderful thing is that if we do what is not expected and do it out of a depth of conviction, people will begin to ask questions. Why do you do what you are doing? Must you do this? Why?

I was a conscientious objector to war in the Second World War and was assigned to work in a hospital as an orderly. But all the nurses, doctors, and patients knew that it was unusual for a person my age not to be drafted to serve in the army. People would constantly stop to ask, "How come you are here?" My answer pleased some and

_____

_____

_____

9. How is answering with gentleness similar to earlier statements of purpose? Notice 2:12; 3:1; 2:15.

_____

_____

_____

10. How does the writer sum up what he has just said in 3:13-16 (3:17)?

The example of Christ (3:18)
Once again the author points to the example of Christ. (See 2:20f.) He now shows Christ as an example for us in suffering unjustly. This is a difficult passage and care needs to be exercised in interpreting it. We should avoid overinterpreting what is at best hinted at but never fully clarified by the author. We may not know enough about the meaning of these concepts to be dogmatic in interpreting them. Some things, however, are clearly stated.

1. What three things does verse 18 state clearly and plainly about Jesus (3:18)?

a. _____ (Compare Heb. 10:10; 9:28.)

b. _____ (Compare Rom. 5:19; 1 Pet. 2:22-25.)

c. _____ (Compare 2 Cor. 5:18.)

2. The resurrection of Jesus was seen in 1:3 as the basis for Christian hope. How does the author speak about the resurrection in the last part of verse 18?

_____

_____

3. Read 3:18-22. List some of the things you understand and list the things that seem unclear to you.

really made others angry. But it was an opportunity to state a reason for my faith and action.

We should be prepared to give an answer for our faith not only in unusual situations but every day, wherever we are, and in whatever we are doing.

What kind of an answer do we give?

The apostle does not tell us what to say but he does speak to the way in which we answer when asked about our faith.

The first thing to note is that we should respect the full personhood of the one who asks. Don't talk down to people or brush them aside. Each person ought to be treated with gentleness and respect.

The other is to speak out of a deep inner integrity. We are to keep our consciences clear so that a yes is yes and a no is no. In this way, even the unfriendly questioner will receive something positive.

Christ's example

Once again the apostle points to the example of Christ. He voluntarily accepted suffering and death even though he himself said that he could call down legions of angels (Matt. 26:53). His love for persons did not turn to forms of compulsion when they were no longer kind to him. Even while hanging on the cross, he prayed for those who crucified him and asked that they be forgiven. No one else carried out Jesus' own advice as fully as he did when he enjoined the disciples to "love your enemies and pray for those who persecute you and to bless those who curse you and do good to those who hate you (Matt. 5:44f).

Preached to the spirits in prison

The reference to Christ preaching to the spirits in prison is found only in 1 Peter 3:19 and 4:6. What does this passage say and what does it not say?

_____   _____

_____   _____

_____   _____

4. What could the writer mean by Christ preaching to the spirits in prison?

_____

_____

_____

5. What is the point of the comparison made between Noah's time and our time (3:19-21)?

_____

_____

6. How does baptism save you by the resurrection (3:21)?

_____

_____

7. How is Christ described in 3:22?

_____

_____

Implications of Christ's suffering (4:1-6)
The main emphasis in 3:18-22 was on Christ's example in suffering. He suffered for those who were sinful and reconciled them to God. He was just and righteous and obedient to the will of God in all things and yet he submitted to unbelievable suffering. The author now seeks to spell out what this means for the Christians—a meaning summed up in Jesus' words in John 15:18, "If the world hates you, keep in mind that it hated me first."
1. What is the first implication of Christ's suffering as seen in verse 4:1?

Augustine believed that it referred to the spirits of the
unbelievers in the time of Noah. They were in the prison
of their sin and ignorance and the spirit of the preexist-
ent Christ preached to them through Noah. (Cf. 1:11.)
But this is not what the text says, for it refers to what
Jesus does after his death.

Others have suggested that the spirits in prison represent the fallen angels and demons of the time of Noah.
But we do not hear any place else in the New Testament
that the gospel will be preached to the fallen angels.

It is also difficult to believe that it means that if people
do not accept Christ in life they will have this opportunity after death, a kind of second chance.

But what then does it mean? We can only point in a
direction in which we might search for an answer.

1. It is generally assumed in the New Testament that
Jesus, in his death, also entered the abode of the dead as
do other people (Matt. 12:40; Acts 2:27; Heb. 13:20).

2. Only 1 Peter 3:19 and 4:6 speak about Jesus' work
with the spirits in prison. (Not Rom. 10:7; Eph. 4:8-10;
nor Rev. 1:18 nor Matt. 16:18.)

3. No explanation is given about this action of Jesus.
It must have been known to the people of his day. They
must have understood it. The problem is *we* are not familiar with it.

4. The content preached could not be different from
the gospel about Jesus Christ. All who will be saved will
be saved by grace and on the basis of Christ's sacrificial
death.

5. The most likely interpretation is to regard "made
alive by the Spirit" (v. 18) to refer to the resurrection of
Jesus. What follows in verse 19 is then Christ's proclama-
tion of his victory over sin and death.

Since Christ suffered
This begins to sound familiar but with a slightly different emphasis. Previous verses spoke to Christ as the example (2:21; 3:18). Now it is stated that since Christ suf-

_____

_____

2. What does the writer mean with the statement "he who has suffered in his body is done with sin"?

_____

_____

_____

3. In what way does 4:2 answer the above question?

_____

_____

_____

4. They leave the things they once engaged in and do the will of God. What are some of the things they did in their former lives (4:3)?

_____

_____

_____

5. Do these things in any way describe life outside of Christ today?

_____

_____

_____

6. Why do non-Christians think Christians are strange? Are Christians a threat to others? Why are Christians persecuted? What does the writer say in 4:4?

_____

_____

_____

fered, we are expected to suffer as well. We should arm ourselves for the time when we will be called upon to suffer. It reminds us of the word in Jesus' high priestly prayer that the world will hate us as Christians, as it hated him (John 17:14).

Ethics and end

The apostle indicates that "the end of all things is near" and follows it with a "therefore" (4:7). This is an interesting way of putting together of the "end" and what this says about what we are to do now. But then maybe it isn't so strange.

The things we hope for, look forward to, and work toward, determine what we must do now to make that outcome possible. The Anabaptists during the time of the Reformation talked about "walking in the resurrection." The fact that Christ had risen from the dead gave them hope for their own resurrection and it strengthened them to accept trials and martyrdom.

Maybe we do not always focus correctly on the end (the goal) and so do not know how to walk or what to do.

End (eschatology) and ethics (what we do) are intimately related.

7. The Christian is oriented not only to the present life but also to the future, to the time of God's judgment. How does this help us evaluate the life outside of Christ (4:5)?

_____

_____

_____

8. In 4:6, the writer once more speaks about the gospel being preached to those who are now dead. Is the passage any more clearly stated here? What would you judge the author to be saying?

_____

_____

_____

The end is near (4:7-11)
In verse 4:5, the apostle has picked up the theme of judgment. He now wants to make some more comments on the Christian's conduct in the light of the "end." End in Greek means not only the finishing of something but also the goal or purpose that has been reached. History has a specific purpose. This goal is seen both in the final judgment (4:5) and the final salvation pointed to earlier (1:9). "The end of all things is near" (4:7) means it is at hand. It could come at any time. It should not be taken in the sense of "immediately" or "soon." The exhortations that follow are given from the viewpoint of the imminent end of all things.

1. List the specific advice suggested in 4:7-9.

_____   _____

_____   _____

_____   _____

Unsurprised by Suffering (1 Peter 3:13—4:19)

3:13 Prepared to Suffer

If Called to Suffer

Assumption: Some will suffer
for doing good.
Exhortation: Do not fear
be prepared to witness
to your faith
Motivation:
will of God
appeal to Christ's suffering
victory to Christ's suffering

Comments, additions

4:1 Since Christ Suffered

Assumption: Gospel
proclaimed to spirits
in prison
Exhortation: Arm yourself
prepare to suffer
have same mind
live in sin no longer
Motivation: Judgment

4:7 In View of the End — 4:11

Assumption: The approaching end
Exhortation: Sanity, sobriety,
unfailing love, hospitality,
stewardship of our gifts
Purpose: That God be glorified
Doxology

2. Why would these be important for the apostle? Why not other Christian virtues? Why "clear minded," for example?

_____

_____

_____

3. What is meant by love covering a multitude of sins?

_____

_____

_____

4. In the Old Testament, the sacrifice brought by the sinner covered the sin. That is, it prevented the sin from working out its evil consequences in the believers' lives. Is that what love does? Compare James 5:20.

_____

_____

_____

5. How important was hospitality to the church in the first century? (Check 1 Tim. 3:2; Tit. 1:8.)

_____

_____

The use of our gifts (4:10-11)

From general counsel, the apostle now turns to a specific exhortation about our gifts. God's grace is passed on to others through the various gifts that God has given to his people. God's work and end (purpose) is being achieved in and through the faithful exercise of the gifts his people have received.

1. What, according to verse 4:10, seems to be the purpose of the gifts God has given to us? How are they to be used?

_____

_____

_____

2. Why would the author call the use of these gifts "administering" God's grace? (Compare Jesus' parable about the talents, Matt. 25:14-30.)

_____

_____

_____

3. Turn to several of the other New Testament references to gifts (Rom. 12:6-8; 1 Cor. 12:4-11; Eph. 4:7, 11-13) and list some of the varied gifts mentioned.

_____

_____

_____

4. In what way is speaking a gift? Don't we all speak (4:11)?

_____

_____

_____

5. Is the art of speaking important or is it the content (the very words of God) that is important, or could it be both? What do you see as the main concern of the apostle (4:11)?

_____

_____

_____

6. Have you seen serving as a gift? Could some of us have a special gift as servants of others? Do you know

some such persons?

_____

_____

_____

7. The apostle has mentioned speaking and serving as gifts. Does this not include everything? the new being we have become (1:3)? in what we say and do? Isn't all of life a stewardship? (The word for "faithfully administering" in 4:10 means to be "good stewards.")

_____

_____

_____

8. What is the purpose of our gifts. Earlier it was said "to serve others." What is highlighted in 4:11?

_____

_____

9. The passage now closes with a doxology: "To him be the glory and power." Usually such notes of praise stand at the end of a letter. Why might the author have placed it here? Could you venture a guess?

_____

_____

_____

Session notes

Session 10.
Unsurprised
by painful suffering

1 Peter 4:12-19

The apostle has set off this section for special emphasis.
(1) He had closed off the first part of the epistle with a
doxology. (2) He begins this section with a new address,
"Dearly Beloved" (compare with 2:11). (3) He now comes
to the heart of his concern for a persecuted church. Will
they understand the nature of suffering—suffering for
the sake of Christ?

1. "Dear friends" as the NIV translates is not strong
enough. The root word here is *agape*—love. It should read
"Beloved." What love is the apostle thinking of when he
uses this address? What depth of concern does it convey?

2. Verse 4:12 refers to "fiery" ("painful"—NIV) trials
suffered by the Christians. But he tells them not to be
surprised that they are called on to suffer in this way.
Why should they not be surprised? (Think of earlier passages and portions of the letter.)

Think it not strange

The Jews had learned to understand suffering. They had seen it over many years. They had developed a way of looking at suffering. They understood suffering in a number of ways: (1) People suffered for their sins. To do evil was to invite suffering personally and as a nation. (2) Through suffering, God called his people to repentance. The judgments of God were seen as God's acts of mercy and grace designed to lead them to a reconciliation with God. (3) Suffering was a great purifier. The Apocalypse of Baruch says his people were "chastened that they might be sanctified." Second Maccabees 6:12 says "I beseech those that read this book that they be not discouraged, terrified or shaken for these calamities, but that they judge these punishments not to be for destruction but for the chastening of our nation." (4) There is a mystery to suffering. In the end we need to entrust ourselves to God who is just and righteous even as it says about Jesus in 1 Peter 2:23 "he entrusted himself to him who judges justly."

The Gentile Christians may have come with less preparedness to suffering. In their history and experience, they may more readily have judged that whenever suffering came it was because of their sin or that their gods were no longer interested in them. Perhaps they felt they

3. Why would the apostle hold such suffering to be fairly normal? (Check also John 17:13-14.)

_____

_____

4. In what are the Christians to rejoice even in the midst of suffering (4:13)?

_____

_____

5. How can we "participate in the sufferings of Christ" (4:13)? Notice how Paul explains it in Colossians 1:24-27.

_____

_____

6. The end will be different from the present. What will be the difference? See the end of verse 4:13.

_____

_____

7. When does the blessing of God rest upon the sufferer and when does it not according to verse 4:14? (Cf. with 3:17; 3:20.)

_____

_____

8. At what times would you praise God that you bear the name of Christ, or "Christian" (4:16)?

_____

_____

_____

just had not found the right way to appease the gods. In any case, it is not likely that the Gentile Christians understood the nature of suffering as well as did the Jewish Christians.

Suffering

The apostle underlines three things once more with respect to suffering: (1) It will come; we ought to expect it. It is not some unusual experience. The Christian confronts the world with the claims and the call of Christ. The claims of Christ on people's lives will evoke the same response it did when Jesus presented them in person. (2) Persecution is a testing of the Christians. The depth of our beliefs and convictions can be seen by others to the extent that we are willing to suffer and sacrifice for it. (3) In persecution and suffering we share in the sufferings of Christ. We are taking up our cross and following Christ. Paul says that if we suffer with him, we will be glorified with him (Rom. 8:17) and reign with him (2 Tim. 3:11). And it was Paul's desire to enter into the fellowship of Christ's suffering (Phil. 3:10).

The way of suffering

More is said in 1 Peter 4:12-19 than that we will suffer. Suffering is presented as the Christian way. It is a calling (2:21). We are to take up our cross and follow (Mark 8:34f). It is simply part of what it means to be Christian.

It is hard for us in the twentieth century to even hear this call. We want to be effective, to be successful, and to do great and significant works. We look for surefire methods, skillful use of mass media, management skills, and if all else fails, clout and compulsion. But this is not where it is at.

Finally it rests on some very simple questions: (1) whether we are willing to humbly but sincerely lay our own life down for the cause of Christ; (2) whether we really believe that obedience and faithfulness to Christ,

9. What does verse 4:17 want to tell us? What is meant by judgment beginning with the household of God? Does John 3:16-21 provide part of the answer? Does "not condemned" not pronounce a verdict?

_____

_____

_____

10. The same passage in John also helps us in the second part of verse 4:17. If we are "saved by grace," what will the outcome be of those who do not obey the gospel? See John 3:18.

_____

_____

_____

11. What does the quote from Proverbs 11:31 say to underline this (4:18)?

_____

_____

_____

12. Read once again the word about Jesus in 2:23: "he entrusted himself to him who judges justly." What does this say about Jesus' trust in God even while suffering death on the cross?

_____

_____

_____

13. Now return to the closing counsel in 4:12-13. What are the two things we should do when we suffer for being Christ's followers?

_____

when he calls us to do good in spite of persecution, is going to be honored by God more than our own attempts to manipulate people; (3) whether we are willing to do right even when we cannot see the outcome of our actions, and simply believe enough to entrust ourselves to one who judges justly.

The glory of suffering

The apostle does not hold out guarantees that our suffering will change the course of history. What he holds out to us is that history and the future are in *God's* hands, not in ours. Our task is to be faithful and obedient to our Lord.

But there is a promise—the promise of glory. If we suffer "the spirit of glory and of God rests on you" (4:14). This is a familiar Old Testament idea. The *shekinah* was the halo or the glow of the presence of God (Exod. 16:7). The tabernacle where God met with his people was filled with his glory (Exod. 29:43; 40:34); so also to the temple (1 Kings 8:10-11).

Peter says that the halo of God's glory rests on the person who suffers for the sake of Christ as is illustrated in the suffering of Stephen (Acts 6:15).

One time word

Allotripiskopos (4:15) is a word that, as far as we know, appears nowhere else in Greek literature. Only Peter uses it. Some suggest he coined the word himself. We have to guess from the word itself what it means. The two parts of the word are: *allotrios* (belonging to another) and *episkopos* (looking upon or into). On this basis three meanings are suggested.

1. That it refers to covetousness—looking upon someone else's property.

2. That it means we should not meddle in other people's affairs. We should not be busybodies.

_____

_____

Looking back

We have, in the last two sessions, considered the Christian's response to suffering (3:13—4:19). The apostle obviously addresses a situation that is different from ours today. It is not so different, however, from what some Christians even today are facing. What does this part of the letter say to us today?

1. What or who determines whether Christians will have to suffer for being Christian?

_____

2. Are we necessarily disobedient to Christ if we do not experience suffering?

_____

3. How do non-Christians respond to Christians in our day and in our society?

_____

_____

4. What beliefs about suffering do we have? Does suffering have anything to do with our faith? If not, why not?

_____

_____

5. For what actions, stands, or values might Christians be called upon to suffer in our day?

3. That it means that which is alien or foreign to one-self.

I would think that this third option is the best. It highlights earlier parts of the message. The Christian should not, in his or her stations in life, be guilty of conduct that is alien to the calling in Christ. Conduct should be in harmony with the person's confession that Jesus is Lord.

Judgment begins here
The apostle speaks of judgment beginning with the household of God, with the people of God. What could be meant by this word?

The prophets had an understanding of this. They saw the judgments of God as beginning with God's own people. Ezekiel hears the voice of God announcing judgment upon the people and the voice says to begin with the sanctuary (Ezek. 9:6). Israel felt itself to be judged doubly for her sins so as to become a purified instrument of God through which the nations would be blessed (Isa. 40:2). The nations, however, will be judged later.

In the New Testament, this holds as well. Those who come to Christ are viewed as being judged already. "Whoever believes in him is not condemned . . ." are the words of John (John 3:18). But there is another sense in which it relates more specifically to persecutions suffered by Christians. The end-time, the last days are seen as beginning with the coming of Christ. The gospel is to be proclaimed to all nations and it is in this process that the suffering begins with the Christians. Read Mark 13:9-11.

Our hope is in God
Peter encourages us to commit ourselves to a faithful creator and to continue to do good. Our hope is in God, not in ourselves, nor in the work we do or the services we

---

---

6. Is living self-sacrificially for others, especially for those in need, also included under suffering as a Christian? Why? Or, why not?

---

render. What we do has to be in keeping with who we are in Christ. But our hope is in God.

Our hope is in God because God is Creator and Lord and has not abandoned creation. Our hope is in God because God is moving all of history to the end or goal chosen by God. Our hope is in God because God is just and righteous. Our hope is in God because in Christ we have come to know God as a God of love and compassion and as the one who raised Jesus from the dead. Our hope is in God because by the mercy of God we have been born anew to a living hope. Our hope is in Christ who has overcome the world.

Session notes

_____

_____

_____

_____

_____

_____

_____

_____

_____

_____

_____

_____

_____

_____

_____

_____

_____

_____

_____

_____

_____

_____

_____

_____

_____

_____

Unsurprised by Suffering (1 Peter 4:12-19)

4:12
4:19

Rejoice in Suffering

Assumption: More suffering to follow
Exhortation: Don't be surprised by suffering
    rejoice that you have been called to suffer
    share in the suffering of Christ
Beatitude (14) as in Matthew 5:
How to suffer: For doing good, not evil
    without shame
    praise God for it
    Trust in the just judgment of God

Comments, additions:

Session notes

_____

_____

_____

_____

_____

_____

_____

_____

_____

_____

_____

_____

_____

_____

_____

_____

_____

_____

_____

_____

_____

_____

_____

_____

_____

_____

Unsurprised by Suffering (1 Peter 3:13–4:19)

Prepared to Follow Christ's Example	Since Christ Suffered Arm Yourselves	In View of the End	Rejoice in Suffering
3:13	3:22 4:1	4:7	4:12 4:19

PART V. God cares for you

Session 11. Standing firm in the faith

1 Peter 5:1-14

The apostle has come to the end of his main message. Now he turns to pastoral items—things which are a concern in every congregation. He wishes now to speak not so much as an apostle but as a "fellow-elder (bishop)" (5:1). He is concerned about the relationship between the "shepherds" and the members of the Christian community. He speaks of it in terms of "elder" and "younger." This is followed once more by a general instruction to all and the final greetings.

Elders (5:1-4)

1. Whom does the apostle address in verse 5:1? Who were these people?

_____

_____

2. How does the apostle present himself to the elders?

As a fellow elder and a _____

_____

_____

3. What instruction does the apostle give to the elders (5:2)?

_____

_____

Elders

In most societies, authority is given to people who have matured and have gained the experience that qualifies them to lead others. Thus age and leadership are fused in the word *elder*. The Egytians (Gen. 50:7), the Moabites (Num. 22:7) and Israel (Exod. 3:16) had elders. Often these were the heads of families or clans. In Exodus 24:1, seventy elders are referred to for Israel. Each city or village had its elders (Deut. 19:12). Elders even played a part during the reign of the kings in Israel (1 Kings 8:1, 3; 20:7). After the Exile, the synagogue also had elders.

In the New Testament, the elders had general oversight of the congregation and the word "oversee" is used to describe their function in 1 Peter 5:2. The activity of the elders is varied. In Jerusalem, the elders received gifts on behalf of the community (Acts 11:30) and took part in the council at Jerusalem (Acts 15:4). They are seen visiting the sick (James 5:14) and preaching the word (1 Tim. 5:17). Paul ordained elders wherever he went (Acts 14:23; Tit. 1:5).

A witness of his suffering (5:1)

Peter mentions that he was an eyewitness of the events that had transpired in the ministry of Jesus. This is mentioned so as to emphasize that he is not only a sent

_____

_____

4. How are they to serve (in what spirit and manner)? And how are they not to serve (5:2-3)?

_____

_____

5. In Greek the word "bishop" and "overseer" have the same root. How does this help to explain the task of the bishop?

_____

_____

6. Earlier, Christ was seen as our example in responding to conflict (2:21) and in suffering (3:18). Now the elders or bishops are to be examples to others. Was Jesus also an example to the elders in how they were to respond to those under their care? What do you think (5:3)?

_____

_____

7. Jesus is seen as the Chief Shepherd. At his appearing, what shall the faithful shepherds receive?

_____

_____

_____

Congregation (5:6-9)

The apostle now turns to the "young people." It should not be translated "young men" because it is intended for all who are young. The same word is used for new (young) wine in Matthew 9:17 and for being new in one of Christ (apostle) but is a guardian of the tradition about Jesus.

During Jesus' earthly ministry and for some time after his death, the gospel tradition was communicated orally to the people. It was important during this time that what was proclaimed be checked for its accuracy and content by those who were guardians of the tradition by virtue of having seen and heard the works and words of Jesus personally.

Style of leadership
The apostle has something to say about style of leadership (1 Pet. 5:13). They are to "feed" the flock and serve as overseers. But how? In what spirit? (1) They are to serve willingly, not under compulsion or as doing one's grim duty. (2) Not for profit. Perhaps the work of the Shepherd is not supported well enough today to make this a temptation. It can also mean that we should not misuse the office for financial benefits of one kind or another. (3) Not as lording it over people. This is a real temptation—the temptation to be "in charge" and to command. It is easy to make demands, it is much more difficult to lead. The style of leadership has to be in harmony with the gospel. (4) As seeing Christ himself as the "chief elder." He is our model for ministry (Mark 10:45).

Be submissive (5:5)
The younger are to be submissive to the elders. Here, however, it is used in the context of the church and speaks not only to young people but to the whole congregation. We as members of the congregation are to be subject to the elders. Again there is a structure, an institution that preserves order in the accomplishing of certain goals.

As explained earlier, to "be submissive" never means blind obedience to others in the sense of not being responsible and accountable for one's own actions. It

Christ (Col. 3:10). Since leaders were generally older, this passage can be taken as speaking to the relationship between the congregation and those who were leaders in the congregation.

1. What command is given to the "younger"?

_____

_____

2. Compare this admonition with those in 2:13, 2:18, and 3:1. How similar are they?

_____

3. In the Greek, the word for elder in 5:1 and the word "older" in 5:5 are the same word. What caused translators to translate 5:1 with "elder" and 5:5 with "older"? Can you think of English words that have different meanings in different contexts?

_____

_____

4. Besides the main exhortation to be "subject" to the elders (or older) what counsel does the writer give to the younger (5:5)? How is this supported? (See Prov. 3:34.)

_____

5. The apostle places great emphasis on humility (5:5-7) when encouraging the "younger" in relation to the leaders. Why would it be so important? What happens if there is no proper humility?

_____

_____

_____

means rather that we will be subject one to another; that
we will respect the way the church arrives at decisions
and will make our contribution to the process; and that
we will also accept the counsel and discipline of the
church.

Yet one is not forced to act in a way that is contrary to
one's own conviction. In this sense it is possible for a
person to break with the structures of the church and so
call them into question or to cause them to be reviewed
and reevaluated. But note the spirit in which this is to
be done—in all humility (1 Pet. 5:5).

Silas

Silas was a leading member of the church at Jerusalem.
He had significant prophetic gifts (Acts 15:22, 32). He is
usually identified with "Silvanus" mentioned frequently
by Paul (2 Cor. 1:19; 1 Thess. 1:1; 2 Thess. 1:1). He is sent
to welcome the Gentiles into the church at Antioch (Acts
15:23-35). He accompanies Paul on his missionary jour-
ney (Acts 15:36-41). It helped that he had Roman citizen-
ship (Acts 16:37-39). In this letter, Peter says he is writing "through" Silas. This may suggest that he was the
scribe writing the letter.

6. In 5:8, the apostle exhorts them all to be self-controlled (again the word is "sober" as in 1:13 and 4:7) and alert (vigilant). Why are they to be so prepared (5:8)?

_____

_____

7. How are they to respond to the onslaught of the devil (5:9)?

_____

_____

8. Does the knowledge that others are suffering the same as we are (5:9) help us in remaining strong under temptation and suffering? In what way?

_____

_____

Benediction (5:10-11)
The apostle closes with a benediction. Notice how even in the benediction the content of the letter is reflected.
"Now the God of all *grace* (1 Pet. 1:2, 10, 13; 2:19, 20; 3:7; 4:10; 5:5, 10, 12) who *called* you (1:15; 2:9, 21; 3:9) to his eternal *glory* (1:7, 11, 21; 4:11, 13, 14; 5:1, 4) in Christ, after you have *suffered* (1:6; 2:19, 20, 21, 23; 3:14, 17, 18; 4:1, 15, 19) a little while (1:6). He himself will restore (perfect) you and make you strong, firm (establish) and steadfast (settle)."
Truly to him be power for ever and ever. Amen.

Final greetings (5:12-14)
1. Review once again the verses that are given above. It serves as a good summary of the concerns of the letter.
   2. What does with the "help" of Silas (Silvanus) mean? Could there be a reference here to his participation with Peter in writing the letter (5:12)?

_____

Pastoral Concerns (1 Peter 5:1-14)

5:1

Elders

Peter: Fellow-elder
Elders: Tend the Flock
  spirit - willingly
  motive - not for money
  method - by example not
    as lords

5:5 Congregation

Younger: be subject
  humility/faith
  self-controlled/alert
  stand firm in the faith
Others too are suffering
May God be with you
Benediction

5:12 Sign off

Silas (Silvanus)
  through him (written)
Mark
  fellow prisoner
Rome (she in Babylon)
  church at Rome

5:14

Comments, additions:

3. How is Silas described (5:12)?

_____

_____

_____

4. What does the apostle say about his own writing (5:12)? What assurance does he give the hearers?

_____

_____

_____

5. Who is "She who is in Babylon" (5:13)? What did we suggest in Session 1?

_____

_____

_____

6. How does the apostle link the church in Rome with the churches to whom he is writing (5:13)?

_____

_____

7. Greetings were sent from church to church and faithful workers were remembered and greeted in letters. Who is so remembered here (5:13)?

_____

_____

8. How are they to greet one another (5:14)?

_____

_____

9. What is his closing greeting (5:14)?

_____

_____

The Christians Witness in the World

5:1 – 5:14	Pastoral Concerns	Elders
		Congregation
		All
		Concerns
3:13 – 4:19	Unsurprised by Suffering	Rejoice in Suffering
		In View of the End
		Since Christ Suffered . . .
		Be Prepared to Suffer
2:11 – 3:12	Being Christian in Your Stations	All
		As Husbands
		As Wives
		As Slaves
		As Citizens
		General Teachings
1:13 – 2:10	Signs of the New Life	Called to Become the Body of Christ
		Called to Growth
		Called to Love
		Called to Holy Living
		Therefore
1:3 – 1:12	A New and Living Hope	The Prophetic Word
		Joy in Suffering
		Born Anew
1:1-2		Salutation